THE AUTONOMOUS REGION

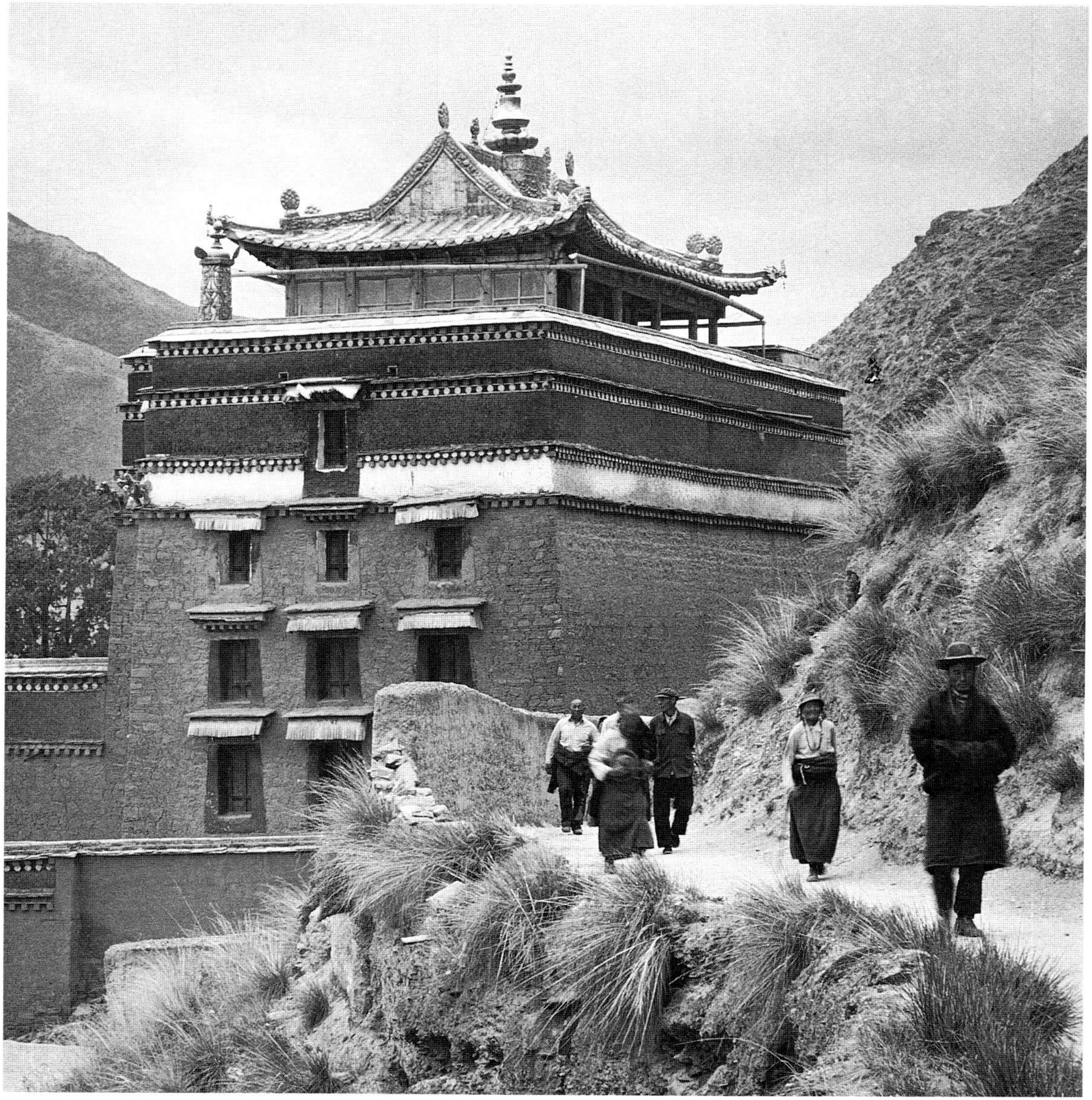

CIRCUMAMBULATING THE LABRANG MONASTERY, XIAHE

the AUTONOMOUS REGION

poems & photographs from Tibet

KATHLEEN JAMIE & SEAN MAYNE SMITH

BLOODAXE BOOKS

ISBN: 1 85224 173 X

First published 1993 by
Bloodaxe Books Ltd,
P.O. Box 1SN,
Newcastle upon Tyne NE99 1SN.

Bloodaxe Books Ltd acknowledges
the financial assistance of Northern Arts.

Cover printing by J. Thomson Colour Printers Ltd, Glasgow.

Printed in Great Britain by
Butler & Tanner Ltd, Frome, Somerset.

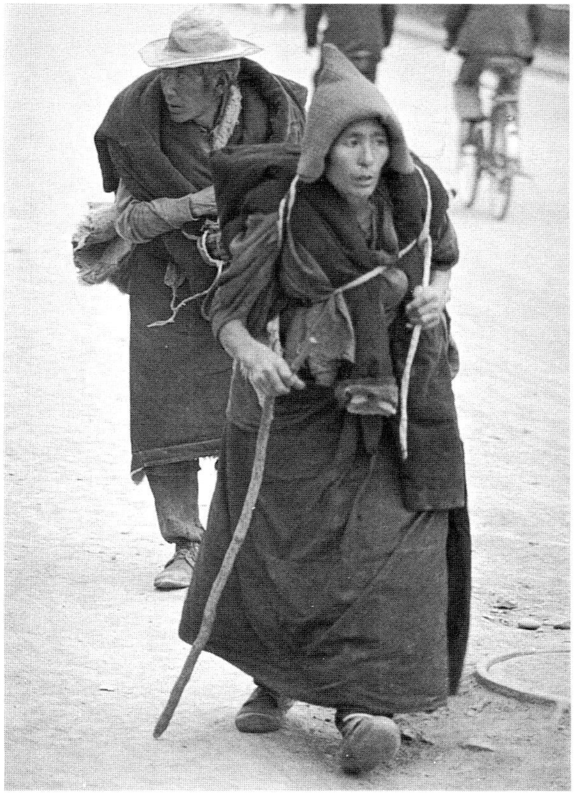

PILGRIMS IN THE MAIN STREET, XIAHE

KATHLEEN JAMIE

On the journey across China I "met" two historical characters. One was Fa-hsien, a Chinese Buddhist monk of the 4th century A.D. Fa-hsien spent 14 years on the road, travelling through China, Afghanistan and India in his search for holy scriptures. His *Travels* are as fresh today as when he 'wrote down on bamboo tablets and silk an account of what I had been through'. I recognised him in the Buddhist and Taoist wandering monks I saw at truck-stops, fortune-telling to raise a bit of cash, or hitch-hiking, or resting at the doors of yurts.

The other character was equally real. In 640 A.D. the Princess Wen Cheng, plus a considerable entourage, travelled from Beijing to Lhasa as the bride of the king of Tibet. Far from seeking knowledge, she was bringing it with her. R.A. Stein's *Tibetan Civilisation* reads: 'She propagated Buddhism among them [the Tibetans] and built the Rampoche temple at Lhasa. They [the princess and her husband] were given silkworms, brewers, millstones, paper, ink, and glass. The Tibetans still didn't know how to write.'

This pivotal woman entered history and mythology. To this day there is a hill in Amdo province called Sun-Moon Mountain. In a story comparable to that of Eve or Pandora, Princess Wen Cheng broke her 'sun-moon' mirror at this place. The sun-moon symbol, like the yin-yang, is suggestive of harmony and balance.

I began to see ghosts, lines of energy and wanderings, criss-crossed routes of travel. Our own journey was halted at the border of the 'Autonomous Region' of Tibet by the events of the time: general strikes, closed borders, and then on 4th June 1989, the Tiananmen Square massacre.

These poems are my hopelessly inadequate response to those events. They celebrate the journey-makers, the seekers and disseminators of wisdom, those who would declare themselves an 'autonomous region'.

SEAN MAYNE SMITH

The first time I went to Tibet I was looking for an adventure and searching for a myth. I was driven by some anachronistic romantic impulse, although I didn't realise it at the time. The fascination, however, was genuine.

I had an adventure and immersed myself in the myth. Consequently I probably missed a lot. Still, it was impossible not to be captivated by the vastness and silence of the land, the glory of the light and the nature of the people.

The second time I visited the area was more prosaic, and the politics more immediate. It was a disturbing time. But I would love to return. Or make a different journey amongst the Tibetan communities in India and record something of their exile.

On both these journeys I took photographs. At the time I was inspired by the simple dignity and beauty of the work of people like Paul Strand and Walker Evans. I wanted to bring something of these qualities to my pictures of Tibet; they seemed fitting. Above all I wanted to work in a way that was open and honest with the people I photographed. To involve them in the process and document something of their reaction, as well as the quiet happenings of daily life, seemed the best way for me to approach this sort of project. Working openly, often with a tripod and nearly always in natural light, I was more interested in trying to coax an image out of a situation than capturing one; in collaboration rather than coercion.

Combined with this sympathetic approach was an attempt to use composition to mirror something of the peace and stillness of meditative thought and the apparent timelessness of the vast landscape. This is a technique that has long been employed by Oriental artists.

Today, however, sadly, this peace and timelessness is being forcibly destroyed by decree from Beijing.

Unfortunately I don't believe photography brings about social or political change. But these people have been the victims of a sustained and systematic programme of cultural and physical destruction over the last forty years. Twentieth-century society hasn't led to a great diminution of oppression, it has merely changed the rules. And there is a great contradiction between the label given to the parts of present-day China that were once separate nations and the reality of their situation. The so-called autonomous regions are in fact strictly controlled from Beijing. It is a hold they wish to throw off.

A comparable struggle for inner autonomy is the avowed goal of Tibetan Buddhists. Their philosophy involves searching for freedom from the constraints and desires of everyday vanity and greed. They hope to reach a mental "place" where supreme awareness conveys an understanding of both the causes and consequences of one's actions and so enables them to be truly independent in thought and deed.

Tibetans believe this state of awareness can be reached by meditation and the rituals of Mahayana Buddhism: the archaic, idealistic, yet sophisticated religion which has been the dominant cultural force in Tibet from the 7th Century until the 1950s.

As a photographer, thinking about Buddhism can lead down some interesting avenues. Buddhism, for its Tibetan practitioners, is experiential; questioning. And so too is photography. The Buddhist philosopher is looking at the "real" world (the illusion of Sangsara) and trying to see "behind the scenes" (to Nirvana) whilst attempting an investigation of the relationship between the two. Akin to this the photographer is also investigating a relationship between the "real" world in which we live, and images of that world, hopefully insightful or interesting in some way, as represented by the photographic process.

The monastic philosophers of Tibet believed that all phenomena, corporeal or otherwise, were related and interconnected. As this conclusion was reached through the medium of the human mind, mind seemed to be the linking feature that tied the universe together. And being human, therefore, was a unique opportunity to experience directly this knowledge of simultaneous universality and individualism.

Their thought was rigorous. There was no recourse to the supernatural except as a psychological tool. Individual lives and the existence of specific objects could be seen as manifestations of energy in a certain form. An energy that was omnipresent yet constantly in flux. (And photography too is a channelled manifestation of a fundamental form of energy, light.)

For the Tibetans, guided by such an outlook, the concept of universal brotherhood and unity was a fairly natural conclusion, and one which their literature attempts to promote.

Their writing also showed that without special training it was impossible to appreciate many of the forms this energy could take. For the trained mind, however, there were experiences in store undreamt of by the uninitiated.

These thinkers understood that the qualities of a thing observed were intimately connected with the thoughts of the observer, and that fantasy and reality would define their different, relative parameters within the imagination of each individual. Similarly, each and every photographer will have a different visual approach to a given situation and will consequently produce different images. These, in turn, will be interpreted in various ways by differing, individual members of an audience.

One thing, however, that is inherent in this philosophy of the ephemeral is a respect for the things of the earth. Animals, plants and features in a landscape are all revered by Tibetans. They form part of the iconography of their inner life. And many of these people appear, superficially at least, to live happily and in relative harmony with the land around them.

Sadly, though, the Tibetan way of life is one of many that is being quashed with dedication and savagery, and the recent history of Tibet is a tragedy which has been largely ignored.

But still, with the courage of faith, the Tibetan people carry a seed of hope and their tradition continues in exile. Their plight is deserving of greater recognition.

TECHNICAL DETAILS

Most of the photographs in this book were taken on a Mamiya 6x6 twin lens reflex camera which I am prepared to carry around Asia because of the improvement in image quality over 35mm. I also like working with the square and appreciate the attitude to working that it helps instill. Nearly all the landscapes and many of the portraits and situation pieces were shot using a tripod and metered with a Pentax Spotometer. For the 35mm work I used a Pentax K1000 and ME Super together with a 35-70 zoom, 28mm and 135mm lenses. I like my equipment to be robust and simple as it has to withstand extremes of heat and cold, a dusty environment and vigorous handling. For this project I have used mainly Ilford FP4 and HP5 films (although at one stage in Lhasa I had to resort to 'Shanghai' film, a bargain at 25p a reel) developed in ID11 or Perceptol diluted 1 to 1 and used one shot. The prints are made on Record Rapid paper using a Lines and Jones cold cathode enlarger and are developed in Ilford PQ Universal.

ACKNOWLEDGEMENTS

Acknowledgements are due to the editors of the following publications in which some of these poems, or versions of these poems, first appeared: *Casting a Spell* (Orchard Books, 1991), *Cencrastus, Gairfish, London Magazine* and *The Times Literary Supplement.* The quotation on page 36 is from *The Travels of Fa-hsien* (Cambridge University Press, 1923).

The authors would like to express their gratitude to the administrators of the Kathleen Blundell Trust, and the Compton Fund for Poetry, whose assistance made the journey possible. They also thank Keith Jones, Phil Butler, Matthew Boyer, Matthew Conduit and Brita Olsson for their support and encouragement. Kathleen Jamie would like to thank Hawthornden Castle for a fellowship in 1989.

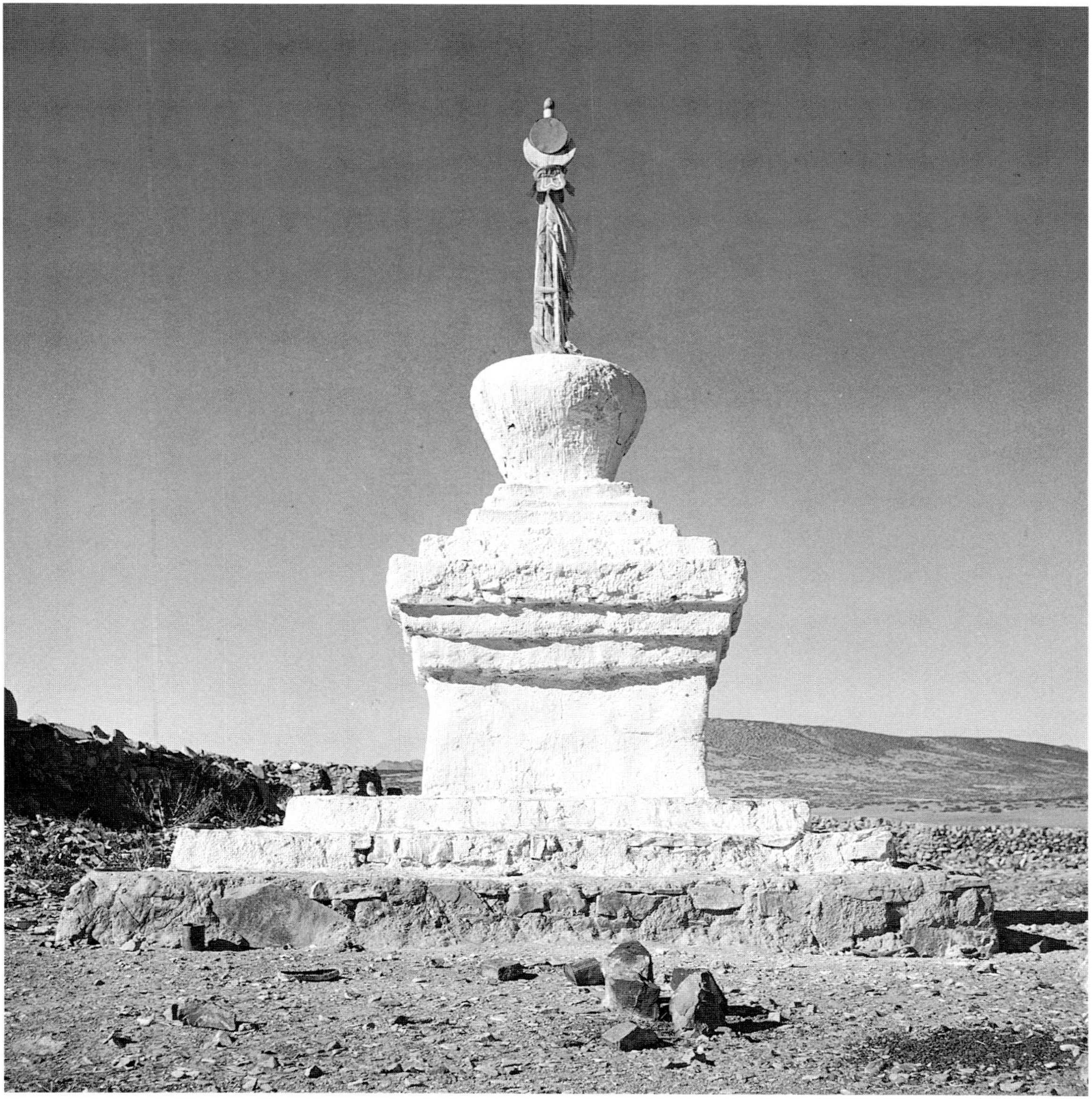

STUPA BY THE SHORES OF LAKE MANASAROVAR, WEST TIBET

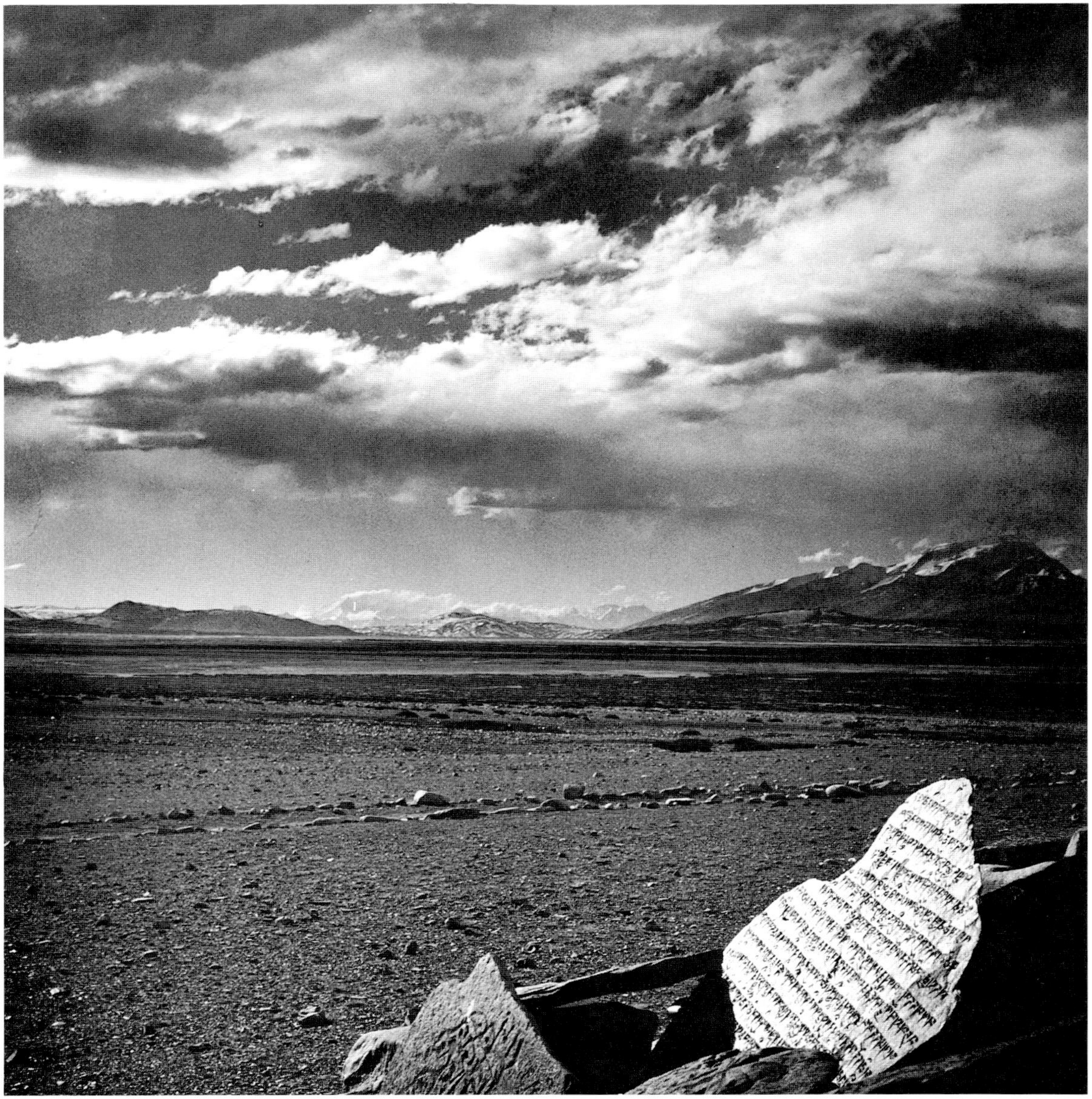

LANDSCAPE WITH MANI STONE NEAR MOUNT KAILASH, WEST TIBET

O a great downward lurch of the heart, as though
he dreamily stepped off an unexpected kerb;
Fa-hsien in the city. He says:
        'Need all situations be resolvable/resolved?'
or
        '*Is* there a high pass over the mountains?'

and hopes/hopes not. Rumour flits the city
like bats, flits the city like bats by night,
rumours on the lips of running tea-boys,
delivered on the hour, on trays like tea.
        And the rumours say yes, the rumours say no.

And with a great shout and a creak
the shoulders of 100 youths
pulled the wingèd city gates, and all
that were going walked or rode
out to the desert before them.

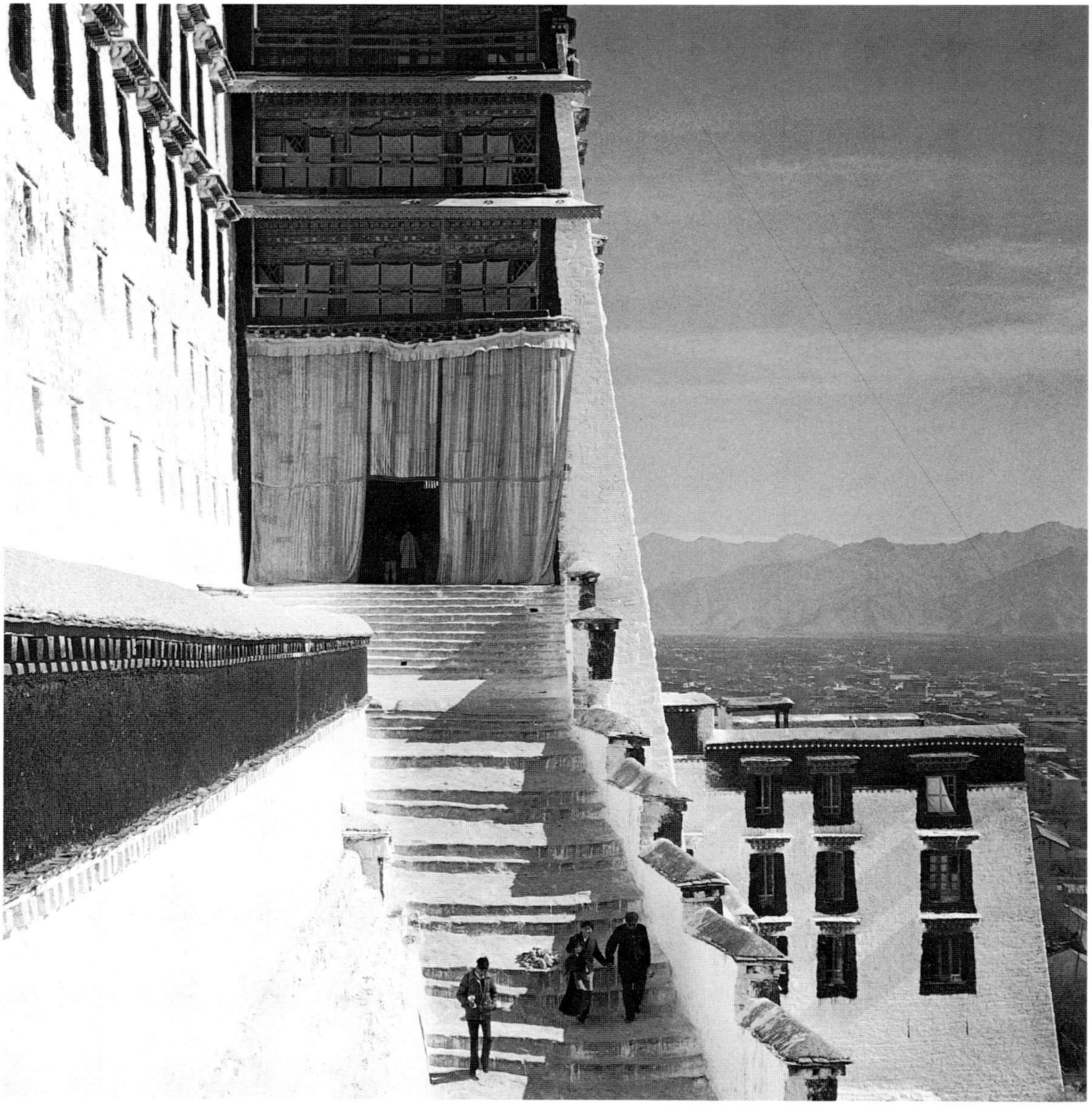
ON THE STEPS OF THE POTALA PALACE, LHASA

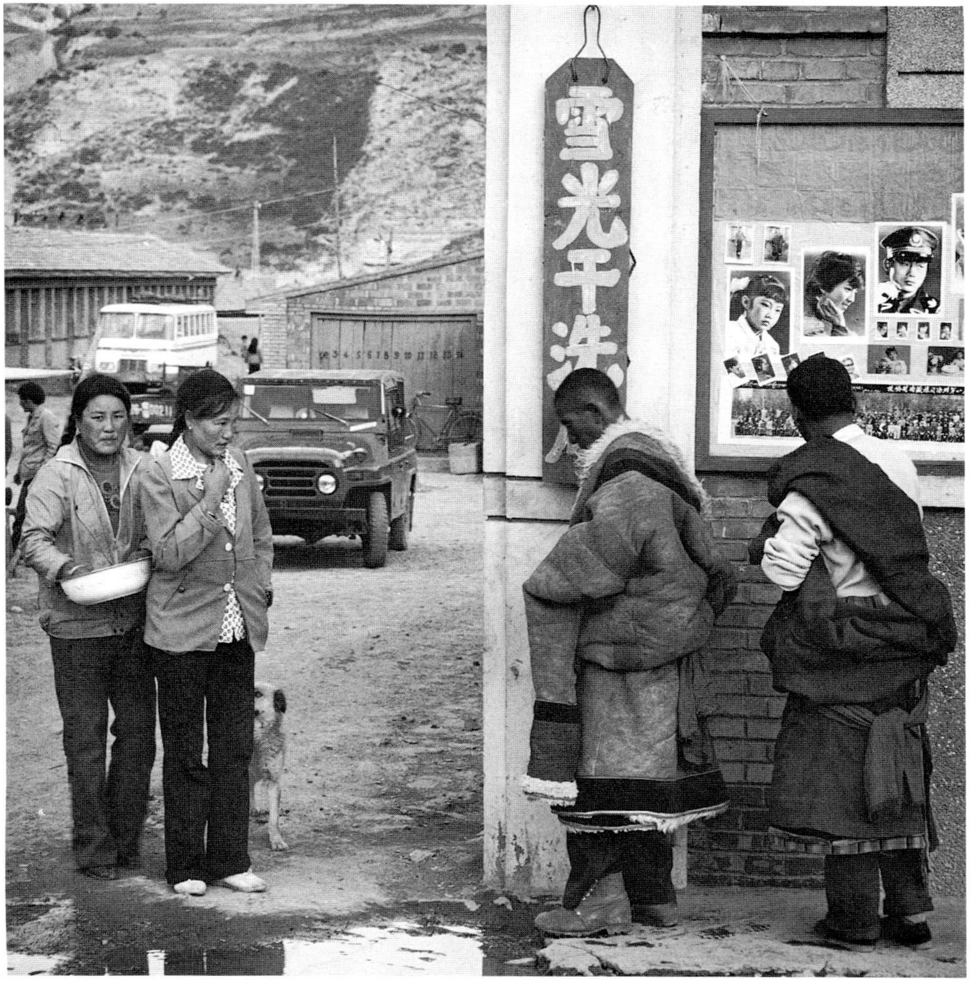

NOMADS AT CHINESE TRUCK STOP, XIAHE, AMDO

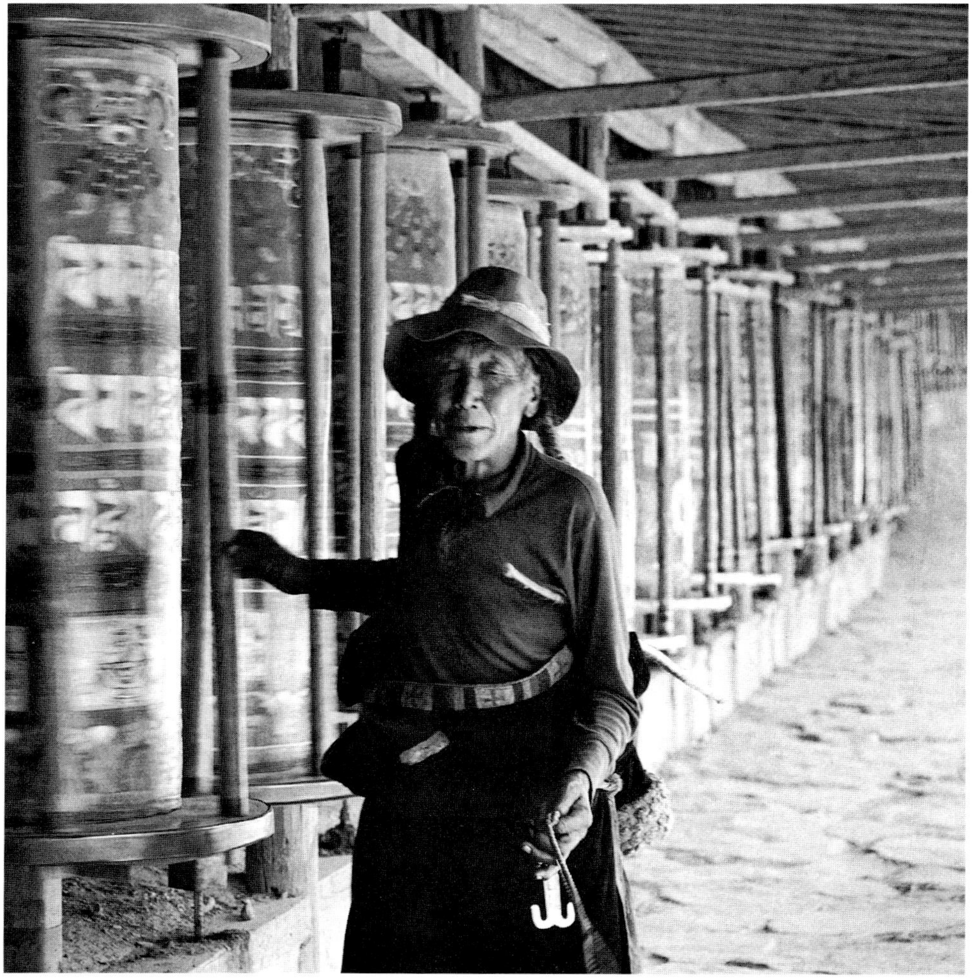

WOMAN SPINNING PRAYER WHEELS BY THE LABRANG MONASTERY, XIAHE

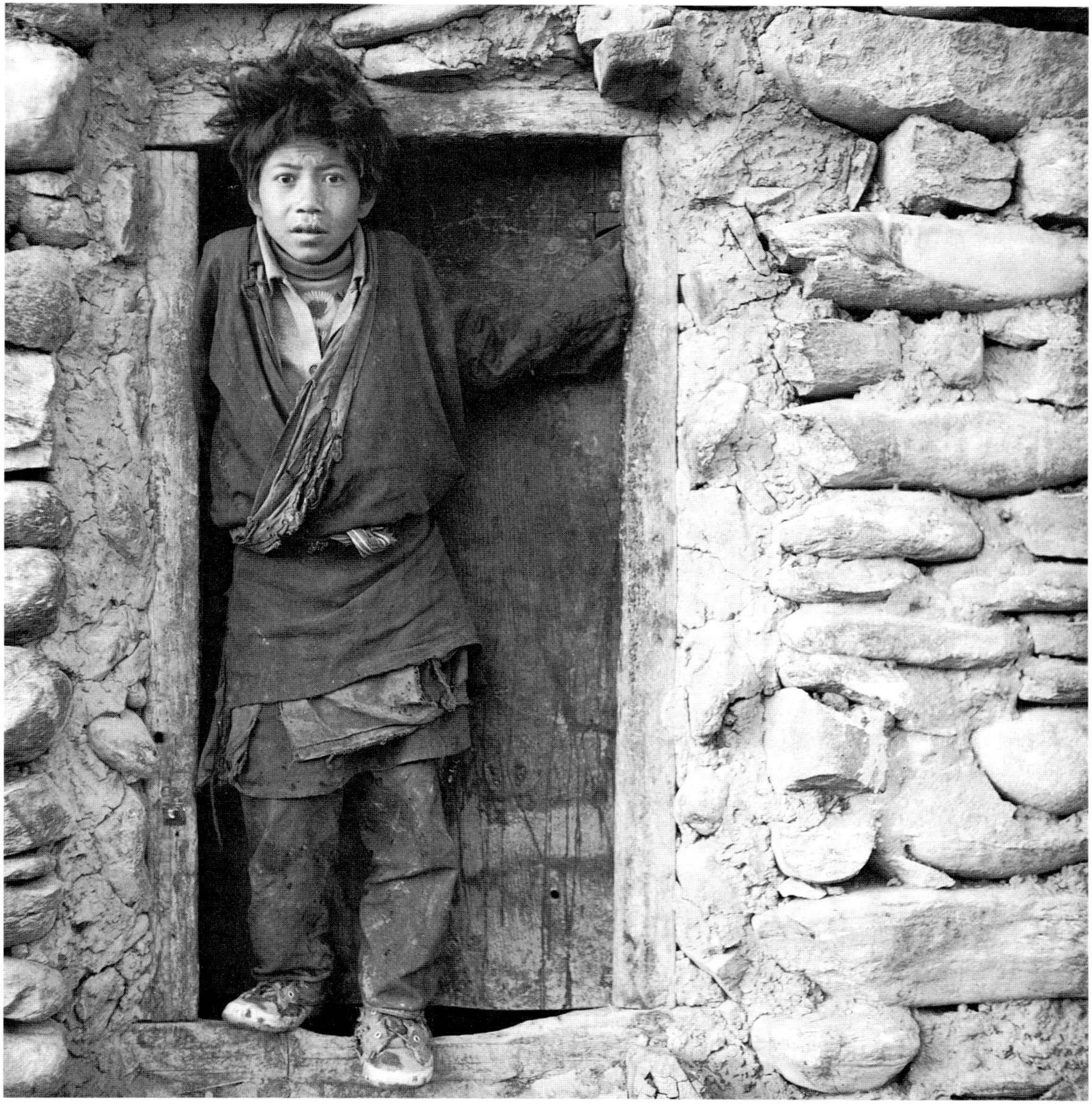

YOUNG BOY IN BURANG, WEST TIBET

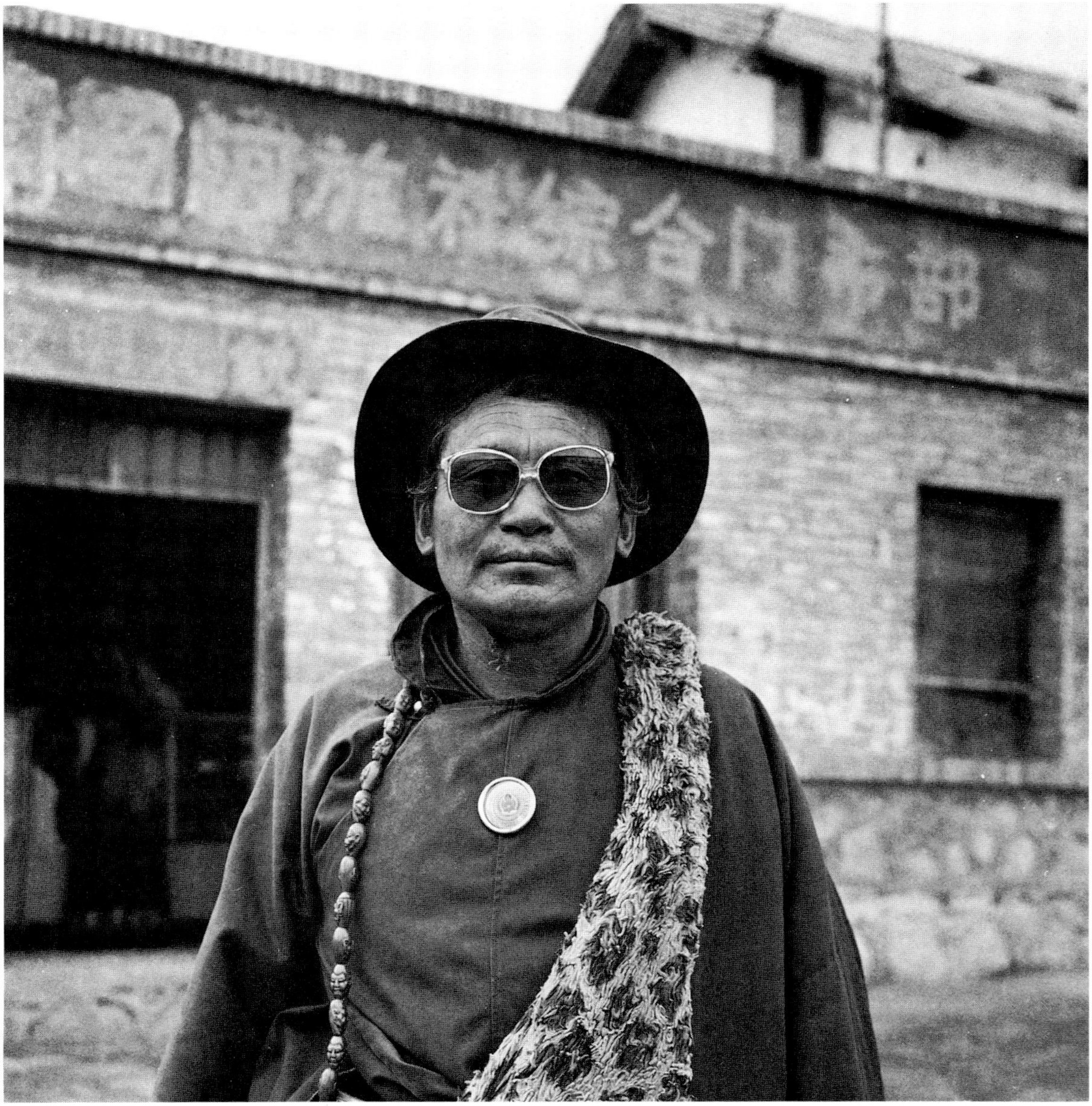

NOMAD WITH SKULL NECKLACE, HEIMAHE

Fires burning in the bellies of yurts at the day's end:
beside a river, such a clear stream there, with a fish.
If he could return he'd return to that river
as the sun rose like a fish behind mountains
and the stream, cleared to crystal foretold.
A purple range to East and to West,
he remarks:
'Not a few have turned back.
Promise or rumour without author or source
ever keeps us moving, against the way
of the small clear river' – which is to say: uphill.
Devotions over, the ice mountains'
jagged edges met his gaze. He smiles, 'Life!
Wo! *That* straggling caravan.' Then: 'But what to you
are the ramblings of Fa-hsien?' Begins to walk.

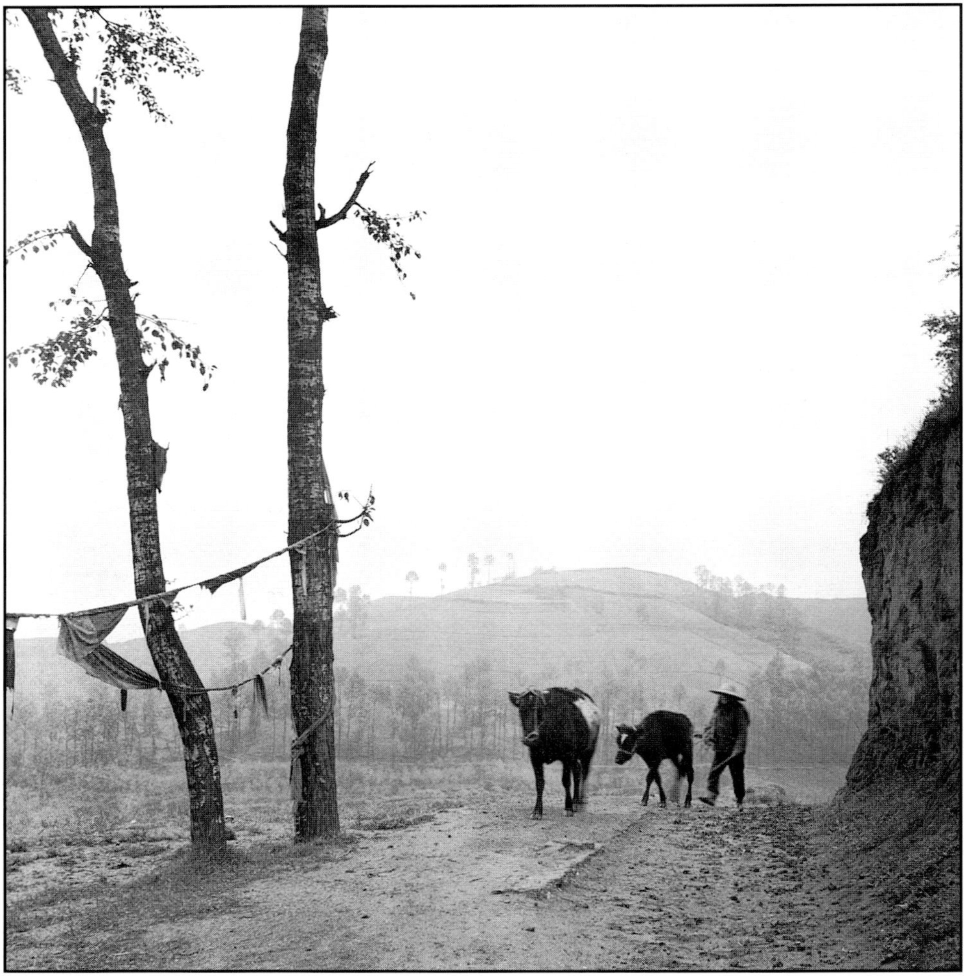

WALKING IN THE MONASTERY GROUNDS, KUMBUM

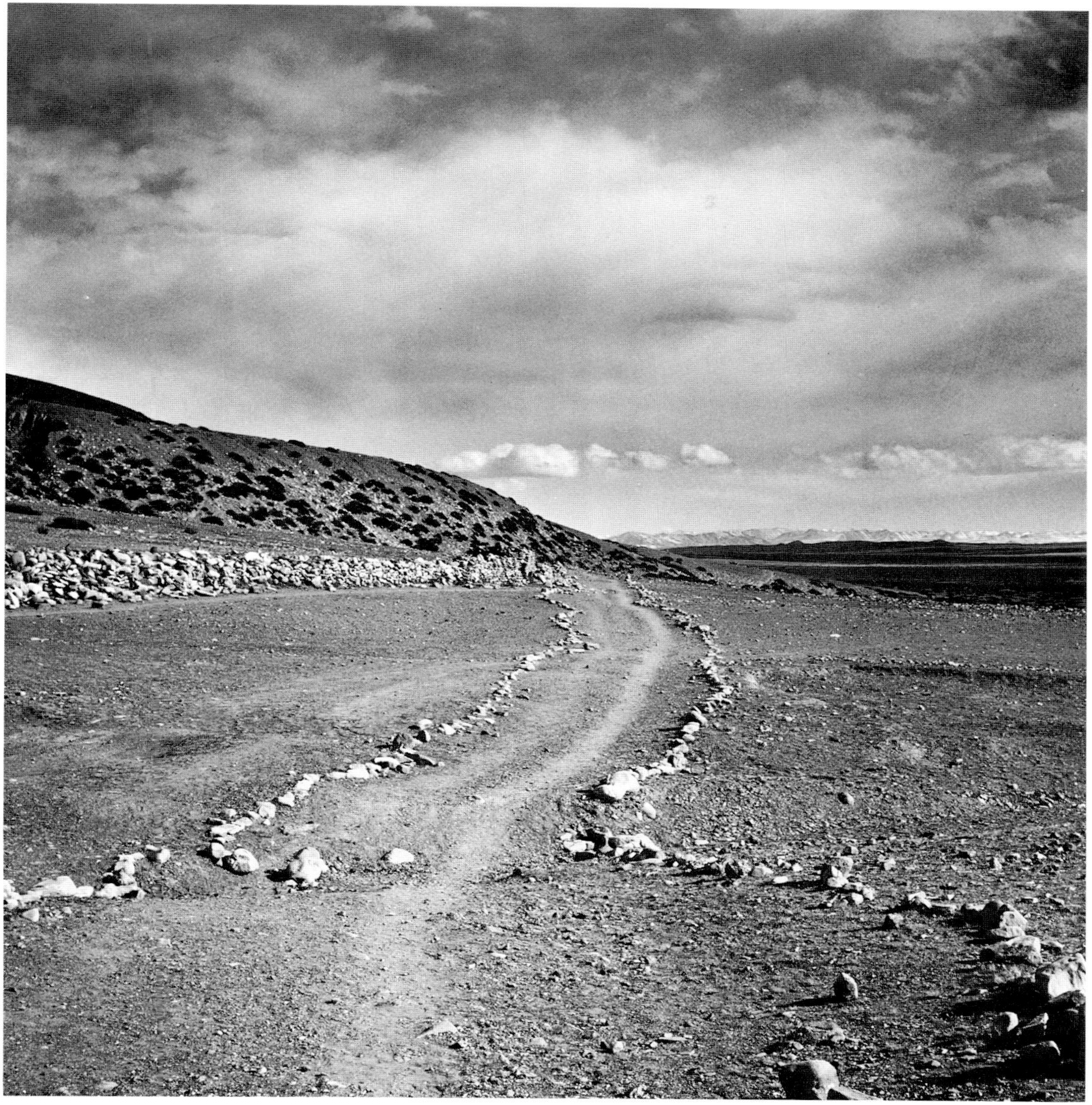

THE PATH AROUND MOUNT KAILASH, WEST TIBET

Walked beneath the power lines
(sagging like pigs' bellies in the sun)
between the desert graves and gravel mounds,
scared the crows with open black beaks, walked
abandoned tar-barrels, wiped the sweat
and wondered aloud:
                    'How did this begin?'
just one tiny act: he'd dropped the keys back
thro' the letter-box.
And though molten tar got stuck to his feet,
all in all he thought it rather wonderful.
He said to himself:
                    'Well, is there?'
when, to others insisted:
                    'There *is*. Secretly, he loved
the way his lips cracked, loved
to feel his head spin, loved
to cough the dust and consider himself
a journeyman, a-journeying.

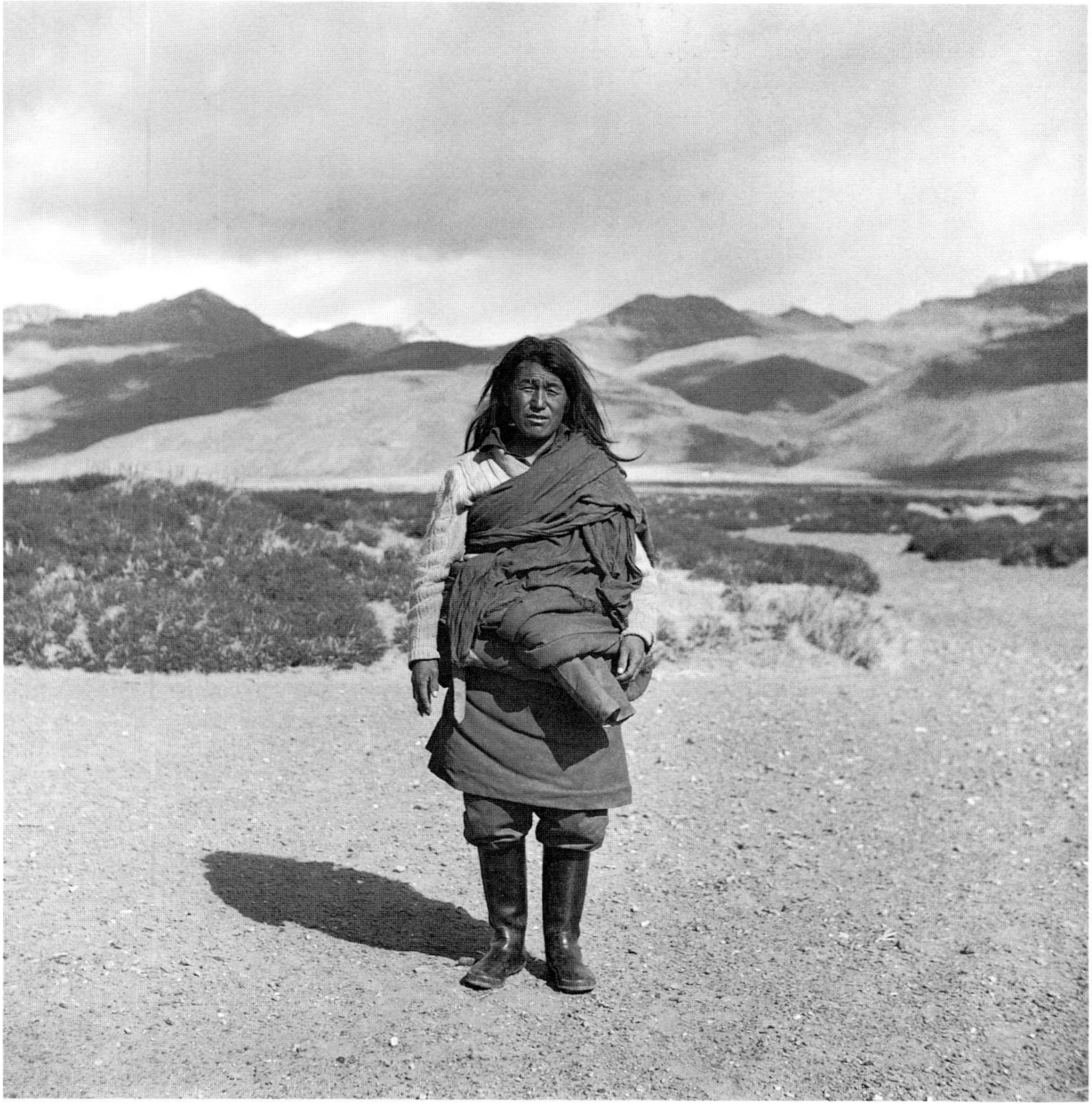

NOMAD PILGRIM NEAR MOUNT KAILASH, WEST TIBET

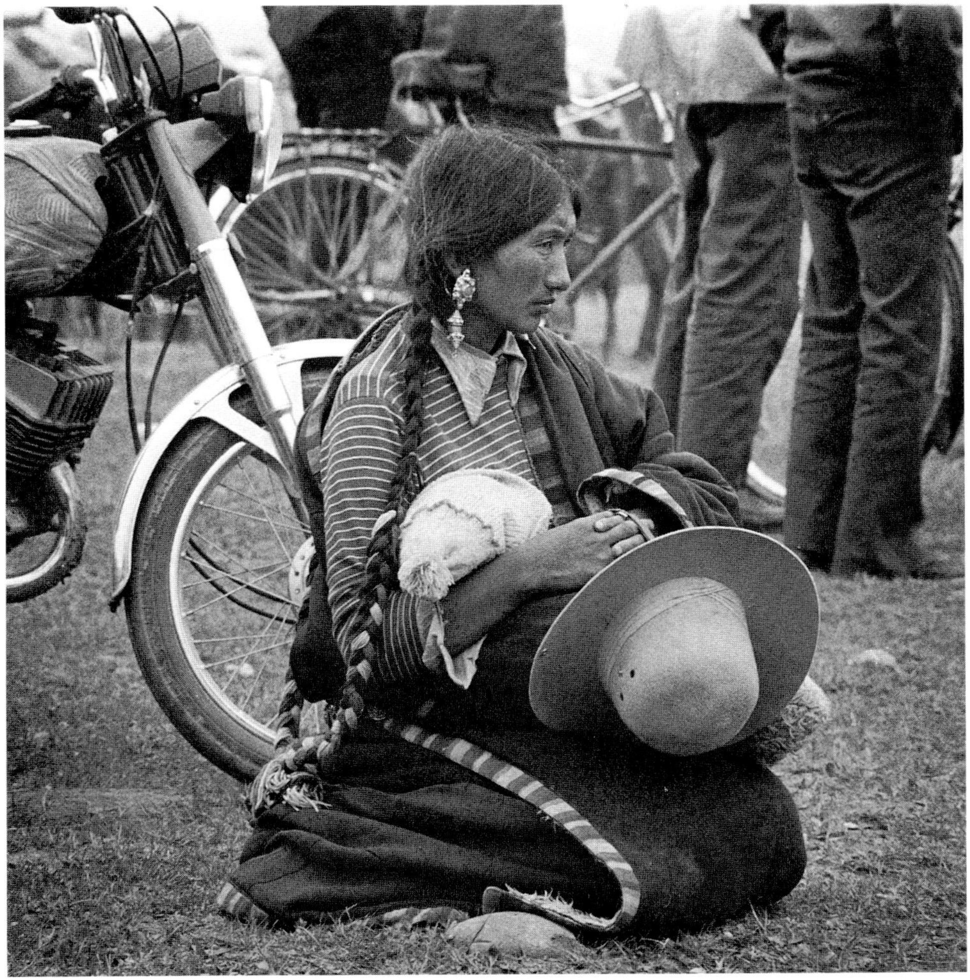

MOTHER AND BABY AT THE HORSE FESTIVAL, XIAHE

Meanwhile, in another place,
the princess (travelling, travelling)
breaks the Sun-Moon Mirror and weeps.

A strong-willed woman and resolute,
she knows when to weep.

The princess breaks the Sun-Moon Mirror

As if a city child knew his heart
could stand no more of this awful thudding,
and in a cellar stale and hot,
black and breathy
as his granny's lap
escapes his mother's grasp
and makes by alleys and deserted wynds
to the splintering gates,
hears the roar,
knows all's lost
                    so opens them.

'What I will I own' says the princess.
Surveys her perfect world.
'A life thrown round my shoulders
luxurious as fur; my heart twitches
like a dreaming cat.'

Dear maid running
with sodden clothes clung to her like children
whose rain-soaked face is like a sister's,
whose company is a clear pool
on a deep and secret river
grasp each other horrified as flowers
and cannot even yell above the wind
sees the mirror smashed at the princess' tiny feet
and on her lips
the beginnings
of a terrible
and mischievous
smile.

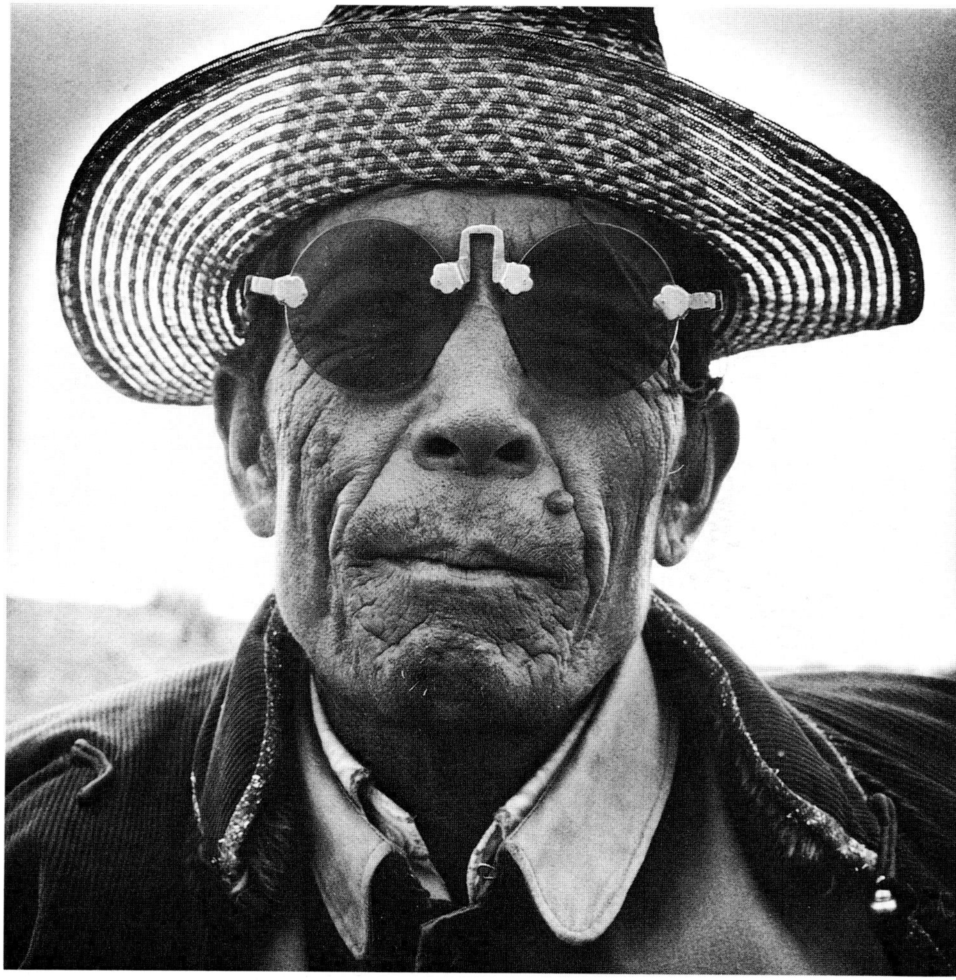

SHEPHERD ON THE HILLS ABOVE XIAHE

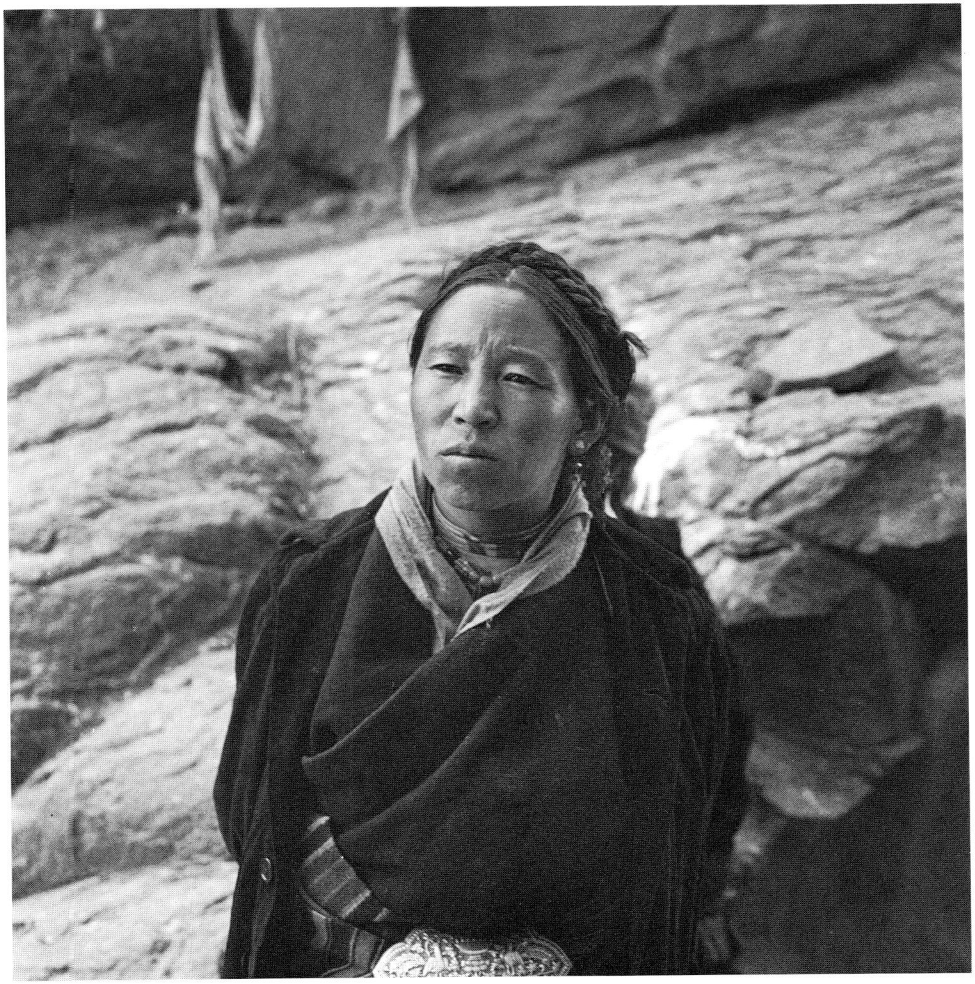

WOMAN MAKING KORA BEHIND THE TASHILUMPO MONASTERY, SHIGATSE

Carved dragons framed the door, fierce and delicate
our house-on-stilts. Creepers chased like monkeys
round our high, half-hidden walls whose gates
opened onto tree-tops; streams
flashing to the village pleased us first. I loved
the tremors that occasionally bucked
our youthful gorge as if a finger
traced its spine. My colour then
was mother-of-pearl; my bed and bedding,
nails, the combs that held my ornate hair…
I'd lean on the verandah, breathe jasmine
air, lean on the verandah, lean and fancy.
But I loved it best when snow came, the distant world
would soothe its troubled self into a pearl.

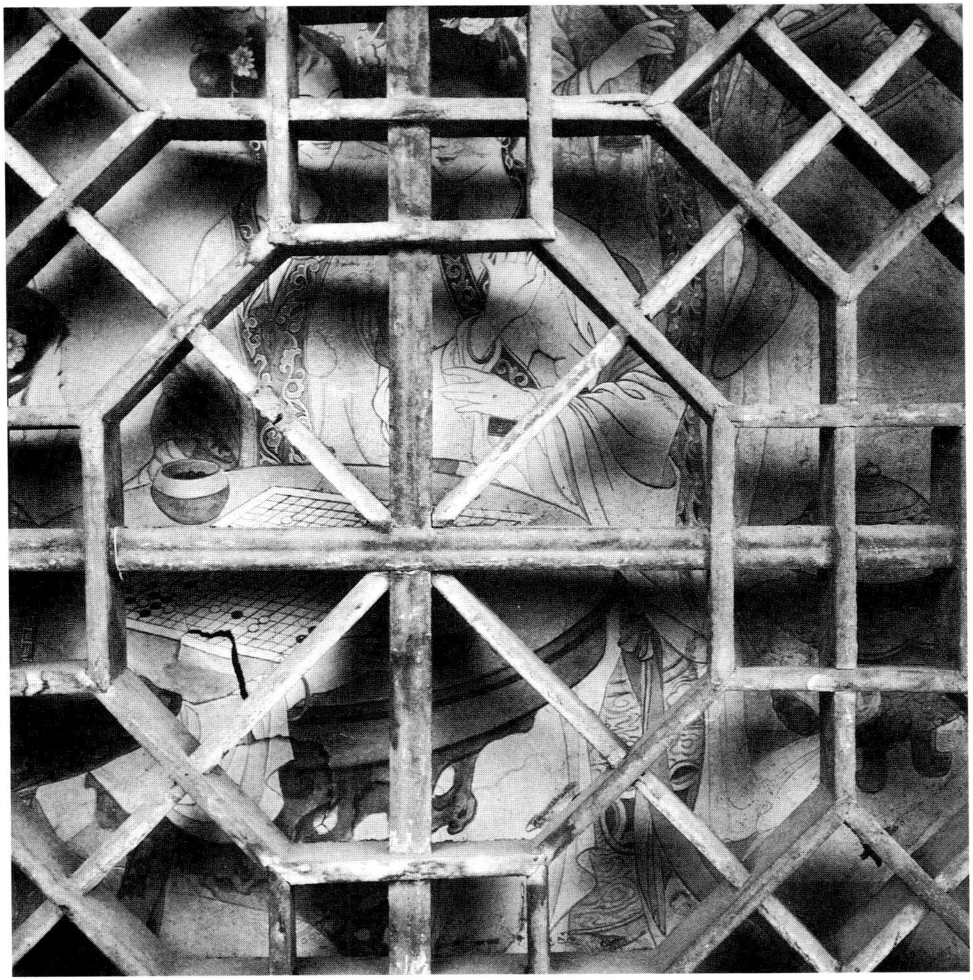

PAINTING AND LATTICEWORK IN A RUINED BUILDING, XIAHE

'The shattered windscreen splits the sun
to a glass chrysanthemum. A few dead buildings
the road's cast up like shells. Your turn.'
'There's nothing here for us,
just a couple of nomads' yurts. Darling
this is *gulag*. Wen Cheng
chucked a bottle from the window,
watched it splash to bits with a certain
satisfaction. 'What' she asked
'are those sacks out there,
ranked like the dumb soldiers of the terracotta army?'
(those that were new were full of desert dust,
those that were old had rot)
'It's the labour of the people' said the maid
and lit a cigarette.

After three days in the desert he came to a spring.
Laughing, grins, 'sweat, mortals, crowd
like wing-torn moths about me'; it was
all charm, the winning smile, laughed
until it fell away in channels; the channels
run to villages, are disciples with news
of glories and miracles sparkling on their lips.
Harvests are delivered fathered by disciples.
For a short time he took this in.
Then it was back to the desert.

Sits a lassie in red scarf,
wi her heid in her hauns, her heid
achin wi the weicht o so much saun
the weicht o the desert that waits every morn
an blackly dogs her back.

And road-builders watch their passing, turn
like weary sunflowers tracking the sun.

So said the maid into her dictaphone:
'Times she'd sit and hum discordant notes
above her walkman, growl
'I'm drowning in this desert' another hour
and she'd mutter:
a girl
could get
bored.

Wen Cheng's
acting up, yes
she's wilding in the dining-car
I hear the
smash of crockery, the waiter
swirling like a matador and fair enough
it's 2 a.m. (Beijing). Now comes she lurching:
'Pass the phrase-book, darling,
let's have a sesh with these dear Uygar boys.'
The Uygar stare at this phenomenon, but
they've tired of their comic books,
give toothless grins and pass the bottle.

So the train bends on. Come the day
the boys and her still playing
paper/stone/knife to some serious arak.
It's a lengthy journey, it's a battlefield;
sprawling bodies stir and find their
rightful owners. A hard-bit woman
sweeps the husks and fag-ends out onto the track.

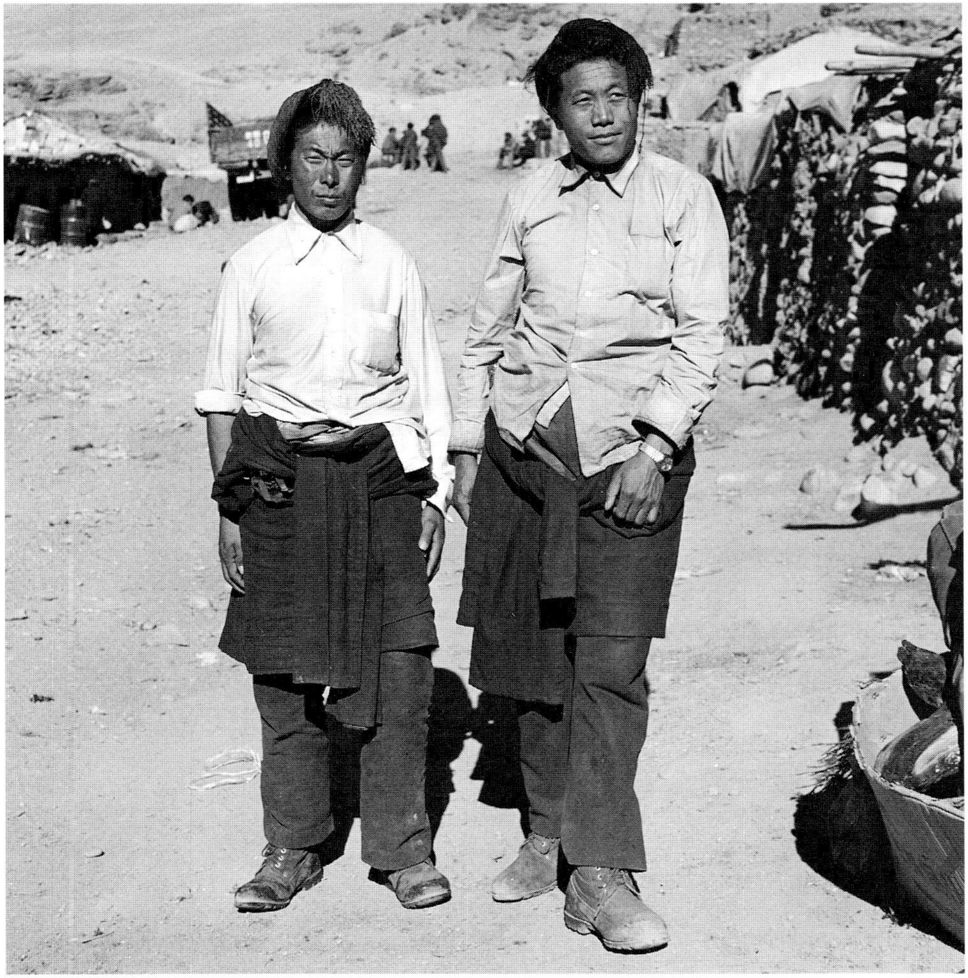

TWO KHAMPA TRADERS IN BURANG, WEST TIBET

The princess rises with all her grace and lurches
down the corridor, the boys discuss
in guttural tongues. She's back:
this time announced
'It's not unusual for golden-hairs
to lie where
Chinese only spit.' '?' I said
'Read it some place' she replied and
took another swig. Her last.'

The party journeyed on for 15 days
in a south-westerly direction
over a difficult, precipitous and dangerous
road, the side of the mountain
being like a stone wall
10,000 feet in height.

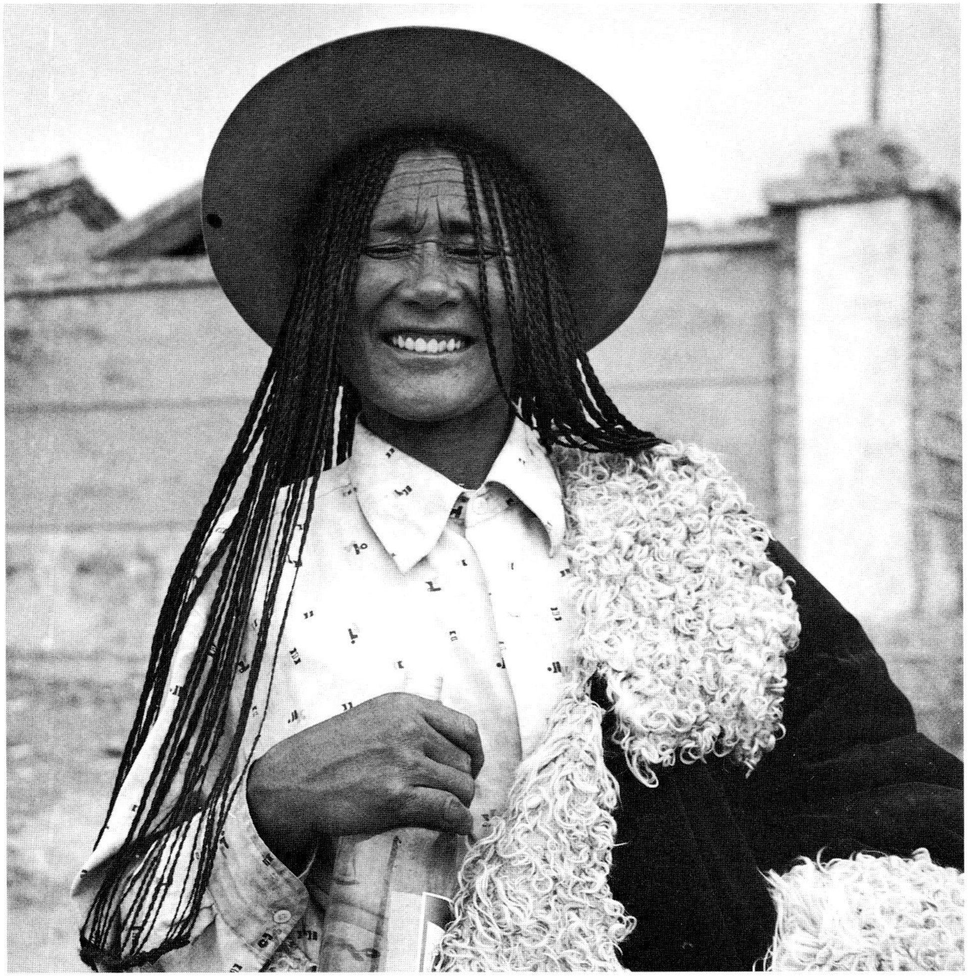

NOMAD WOMAN, HEIMAHE, AMDO

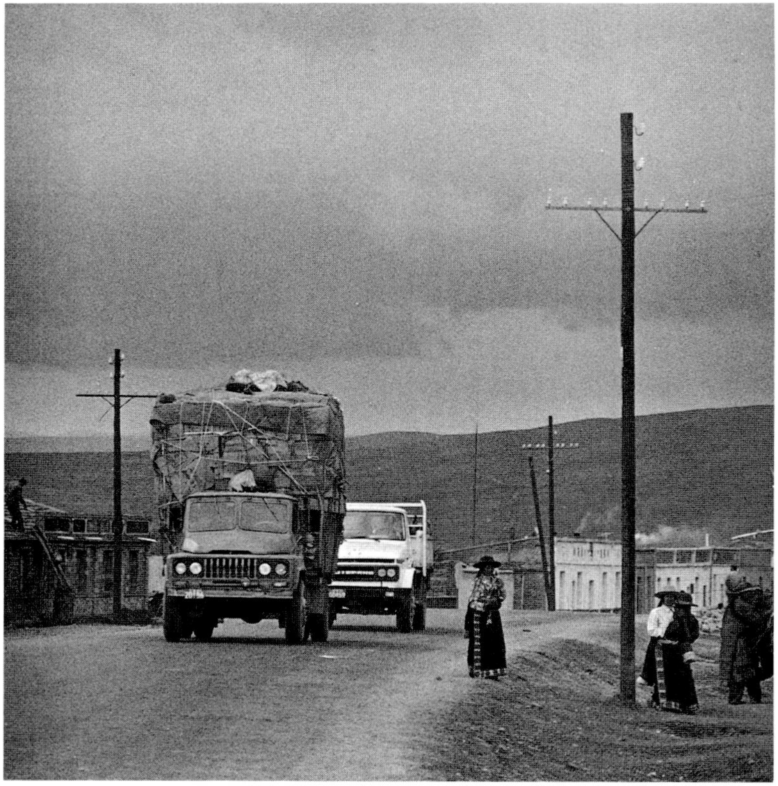

TRUCKS AT HEIMAHE

Unbeknown to them, Fa-hsien,
riding hobo on the box-car
sees the desert change miraculous to plain.
He fancies in the sheep-dogs' bark
a hidden 'yes!' and doesn't half
admire how the nomads ride,
so splits his time, between, on one hand,
attending to the scenery
he's dragged across,
and on the other, learning to divine.

Learning to divine his own future.
He's laying low, he's two days out
heart-in-mouth and hiding from the police
and diesel fumes. It's a truck-of-lead
and slow. The sky's detonated
blue across the day; he stares it out
and hopes, conversely fears and knows.
He feels quite sick. It's worth it.

Swags and swathes of hills billowing o
as a child he dreamed of sailing; the sailing hills;
he hears his heart shanty and shepherds
call like bosuns.
The prayer-flags yearn like full-rigged ships
to quit this witness, earth. He knows
already he's too far slipped
to make the leap ashore.
Aye, it's strange quiver; and he knows
himself an arrow already shot the bow.
He cries, tells himself, as if he didn't know
It's worth it, worth it, worth it.

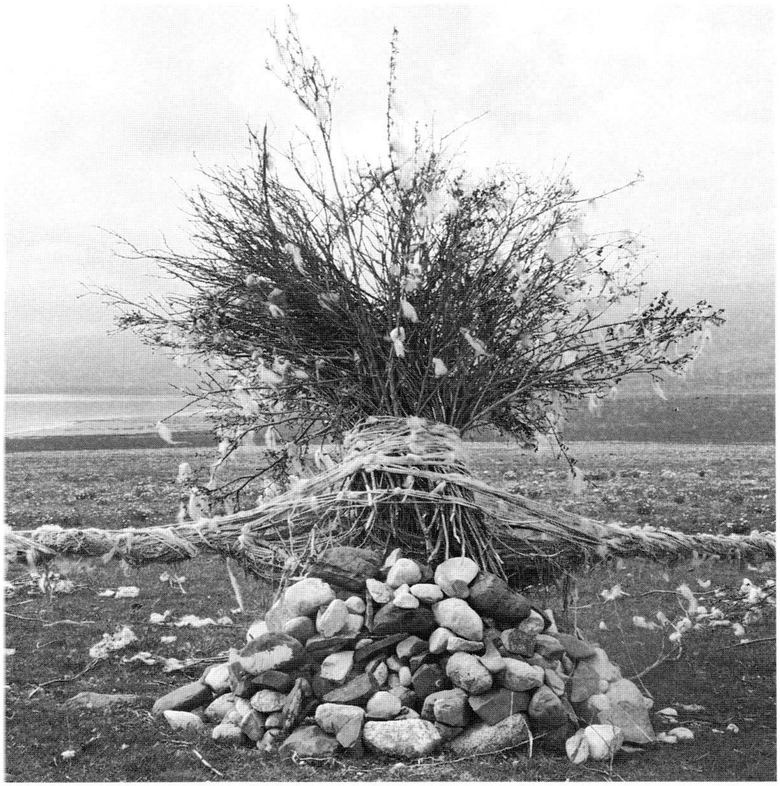

CEREMONIAL BRUSHWOOD STRUCTURE IN HEIMAHE

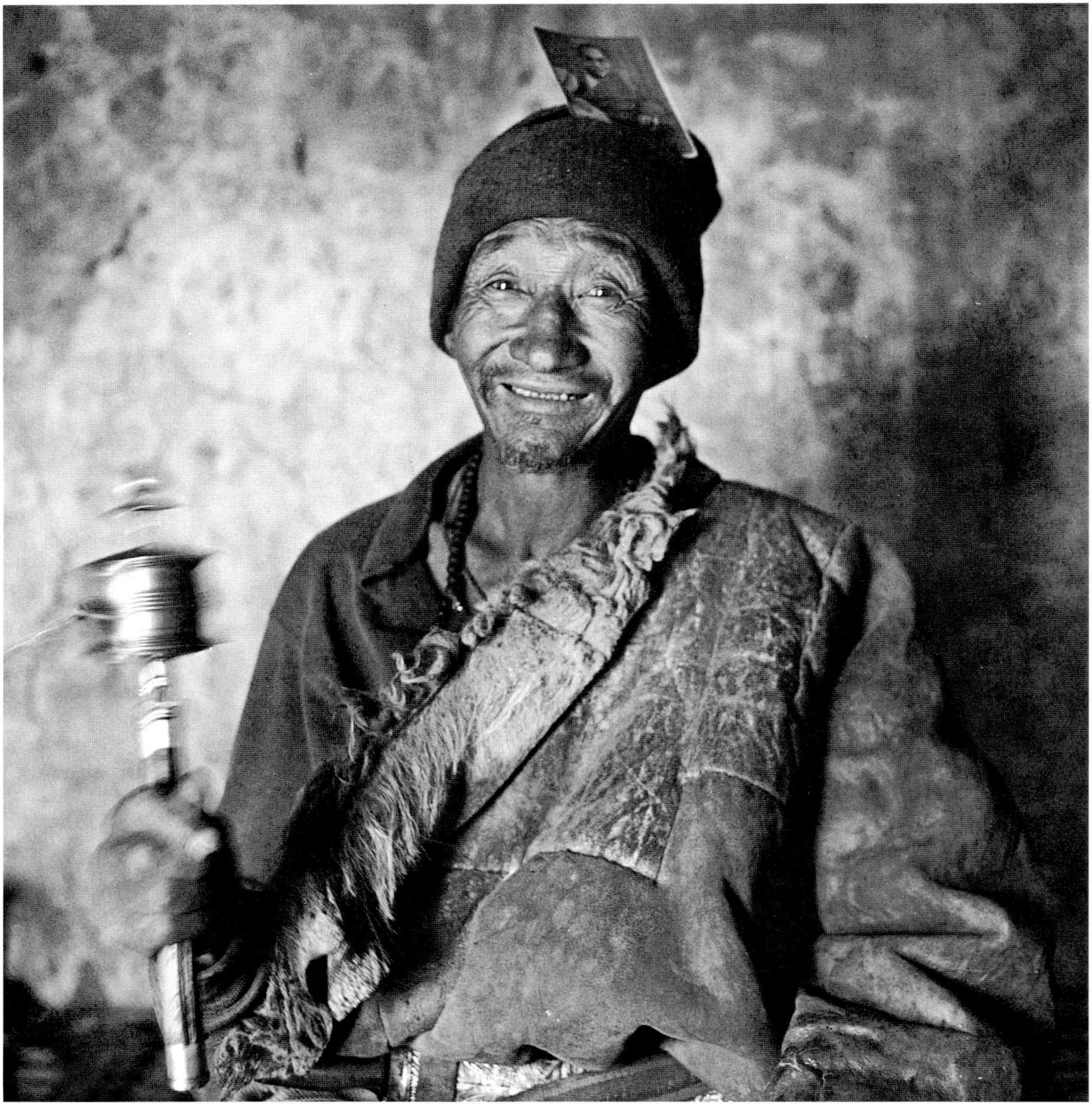

PILGRIM AT TARCHEN, MOUNT KAILASH, WEST TIBET

The travels of Fa-hsien

His bed is hard, his smell
a travel-musk of months through teeming villages.
The walls of course are stained, the sheet
he almost envies: old, plain.

He rises, ties his top-knot, wanders
to the boiler-room, with his
double-happiness thermos flask,
noting
        every vessel can be broken, filled,
and he is empty, these days. Not old
as the sun-lines round his eyes suggest
which eyes have seen:
                        many things out of strong places
et cetera. And who knows what his robe conceals:
tattoos, a bleeding heart.

*

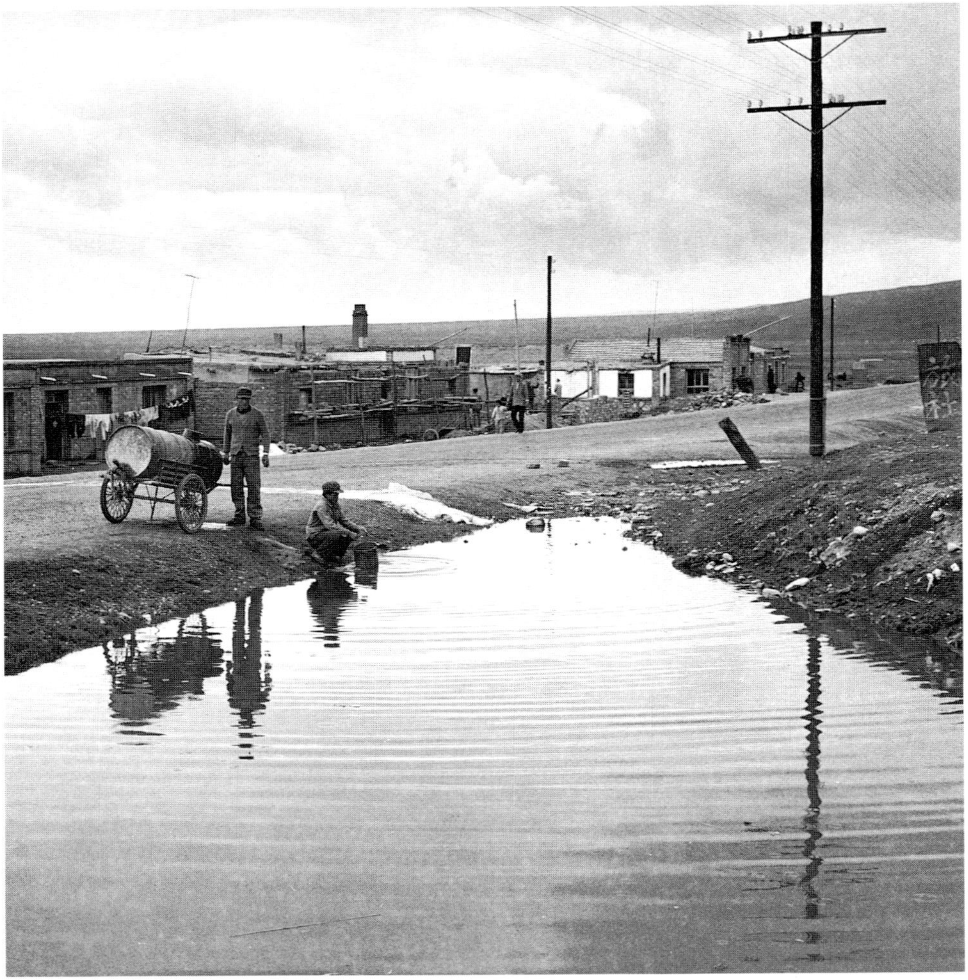

WATER CARRIERS, HEIMAHE

There's roads and there are one-horse-towns
and any climb out of hamlet, gorge or wilderness
he looks in wonder,
to fellow travellers he replies:
'What wisdom have I gathered? None!
That's my tuppence worth', walks on.
'Threw it in a ditch and walk unburdened.'

And also in the ditch, a dog, days dead, ignored.
'I've lied and vowed at umpteen altars,
and know I can be
                utterly deceived.
Perhaps still am.'

At the thin black line of shade at a truckstop
while they fix the fan-belt
and there's no water
he'll bring out yarrow-stalks, divine.
And sometimes, walking alone, he finds
the centre of his being, flinches,
for it's nowt
            but an alms bowl.
Waiting at a roadside, he scratches the dust
with a stick, finds: more dust.
In the hot shade of some godforsaken Xinjiang bunkhouse
remembers the river and the fish.

(o monk, whither do you wander?
to garner wisdom and bring scripture home)

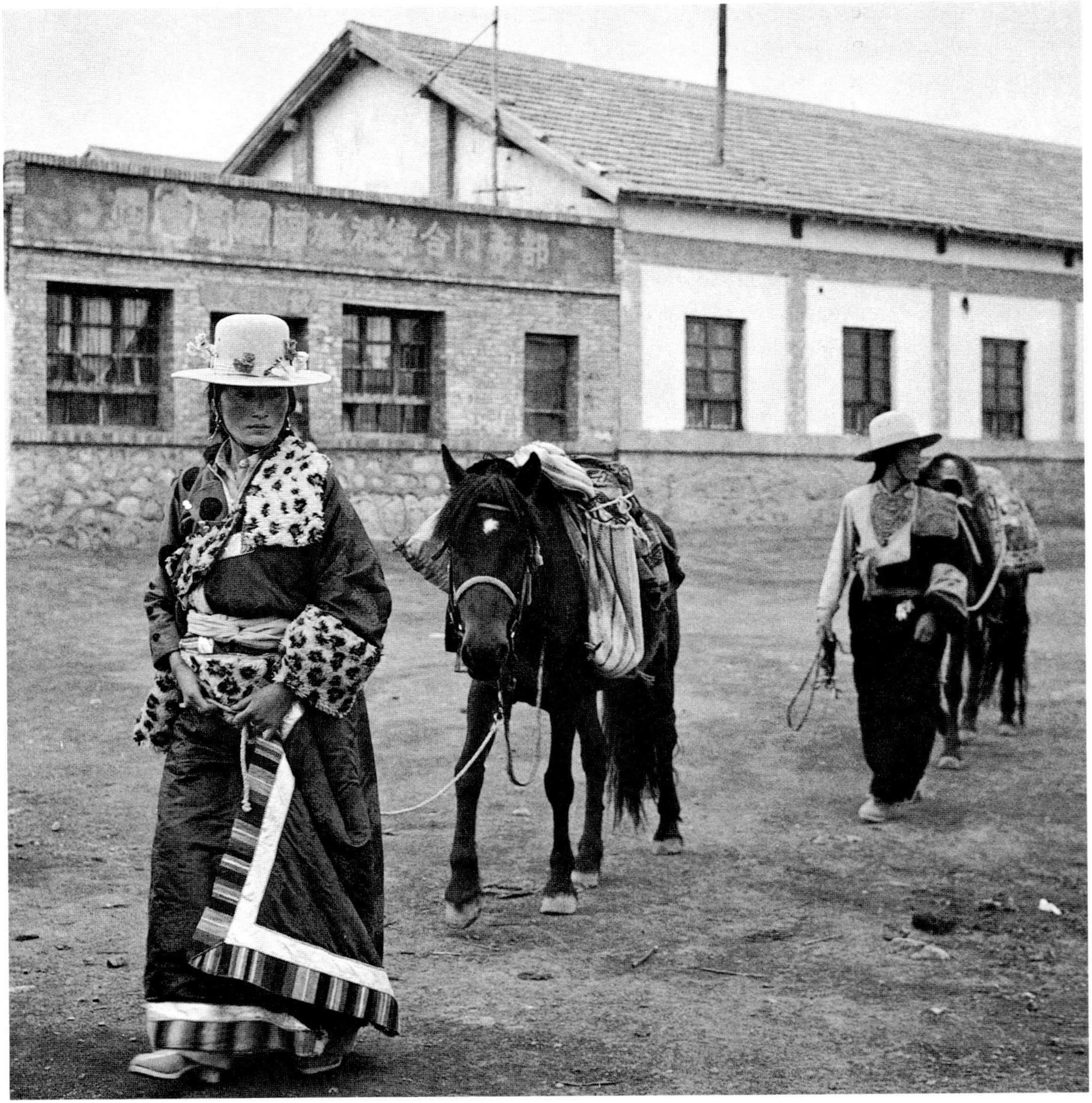

TWO NOMAD WOMEN AND THEIR HORSES, HEIMAHE

Fine horsewomen both and a long time travelling.
Wen Cheng bends low and adjusts the stirrup.
Something tells her this is the border: a breath of wind
from the dark and jagged mountains
a circus of secrets in the valley at her feet.

Nights, and the tents glow in a river bend,
the keepers of secrets
                    together in cliques –
master brewers growing merry round a camp-fire;
thin-faced glass-makers trickle silt
                    between their fingers,
the silk-workers guard their covered baskets.
And Wen Cheng could read the marks of darkness.
O rumour, they have no paper, beer, script.
Sometimes she wonders
                    what kind of place it is she's going,
kicks the horse and turns down before nightfall.

Like the others these days she talks most about the future;
out in the night they're starting to communicate;
secrets revealed and revealed amongst themselves.

We crossed the watershed. A small stream
ran with us down the mountain;
a thumb of rainbow marked the sky.
At the doors of yurts
women and girls wiped their brows
and waved as they churned
summer to its yellow end, a sound
like oars
                on a still and distant loch.

In a purse the mirror's shards
tied from her waist, tinkled most attractively
as we rode; smashed, she sighed
                into this/ not this
                like a common
                        bottle
                        of bitter beer.

And holding the dancing horse on a tight rein
twisted back, hair joyously undone
I told her 'we are tense vessels, each contain
all the energy required for change'
which made her laugh, and I knew
that if her robes indeed concealed
                a little lady's
            pearl-handled pistol
it was for nought
but shooting locks off boxes, prison cells et cetera.

As yaks gathered at the fanks,
like an inhaled breath, buttercups
at their patient hooves
hardened their hearts
against the night. Our running dogs
sniffed a hint of snow,
on the golden sunset
where a lark's black flight
leapt and leapt
like a telegraph wire
on a straight road.

At the shore of a loch called Qinghai we rested,
hobbled the horses and let them graze
the sweet wild pasture.

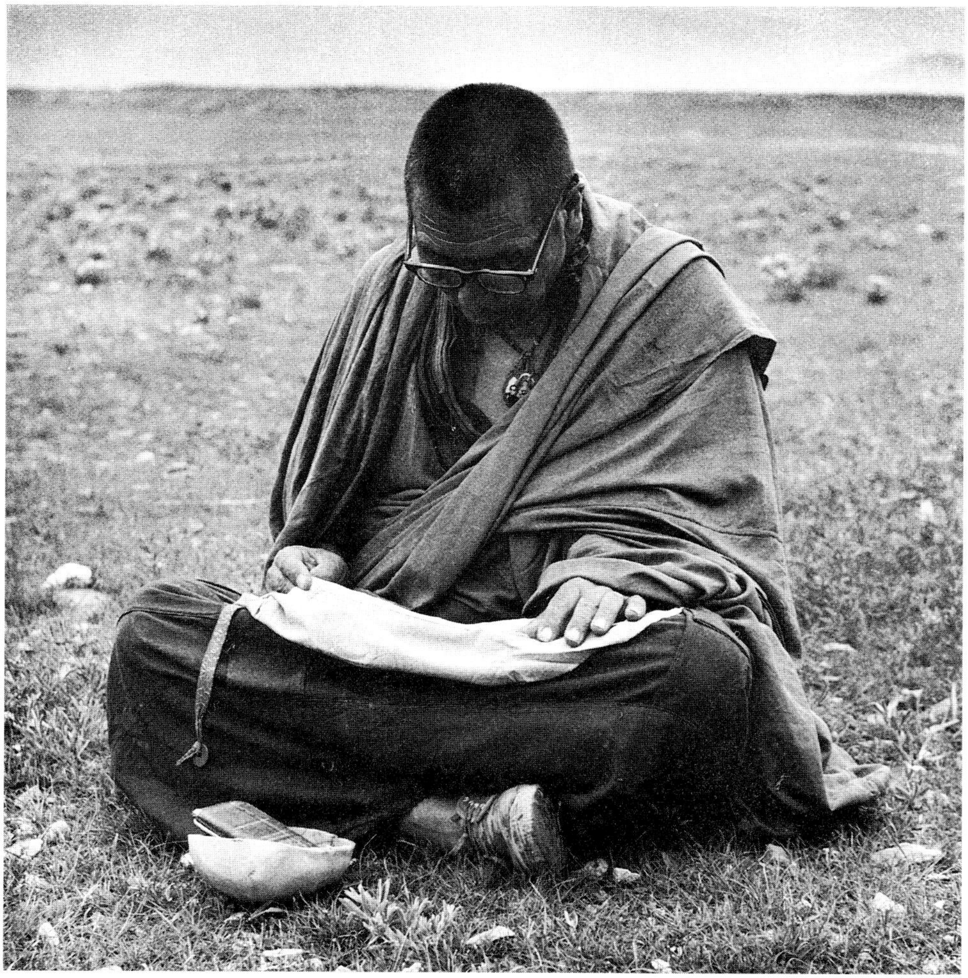

MONK READING PRAYERS BY THE SHORE OF QINGHAI LAKE, AMDO

Fa-hsien, cross-legged in a light rain,
takes his tin spectacle case,
        watches the first print he ever made
(on a lonely shore)
                        wash away.
Though desert dust still clings to his hems
he has bathed fresh and clean
in his joyous lake,
and now his hand and cards have changed,
reveal
a hanker for his ain folk,
                his auld hert follows suit.

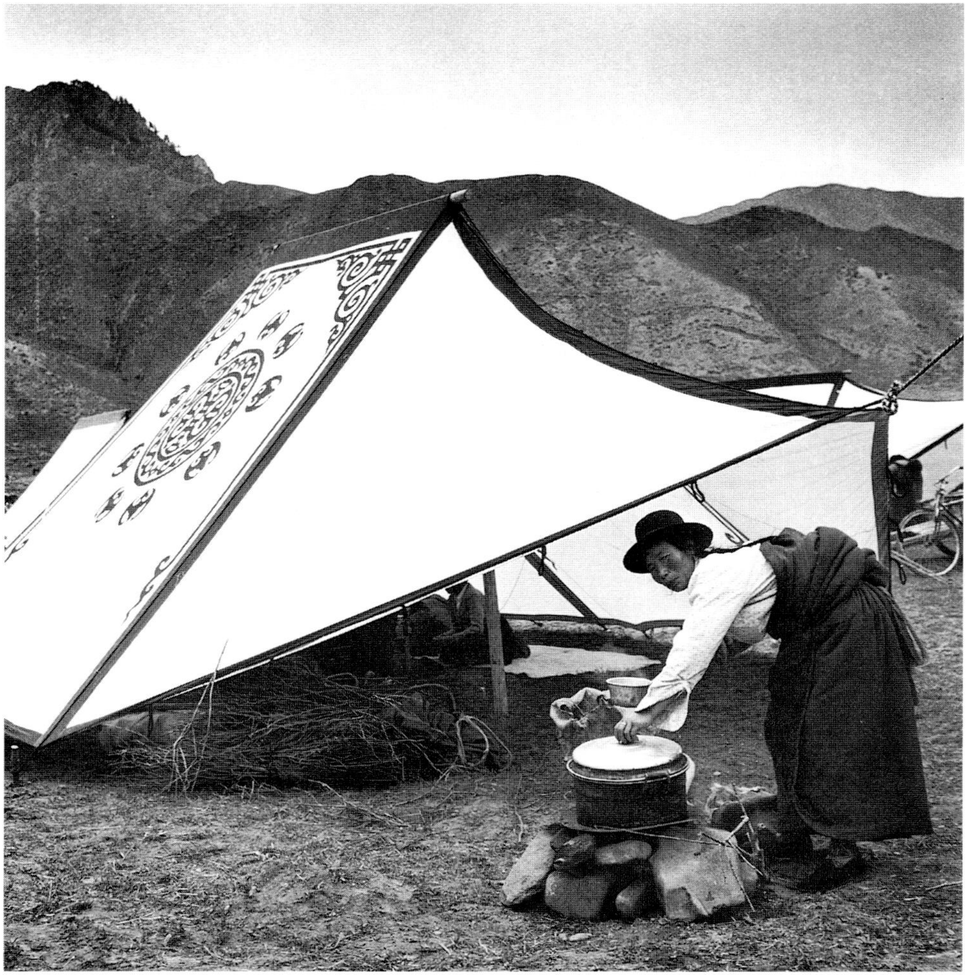

PREPARING DINNER AT THE HORSE FESTIVAL, XIAHE

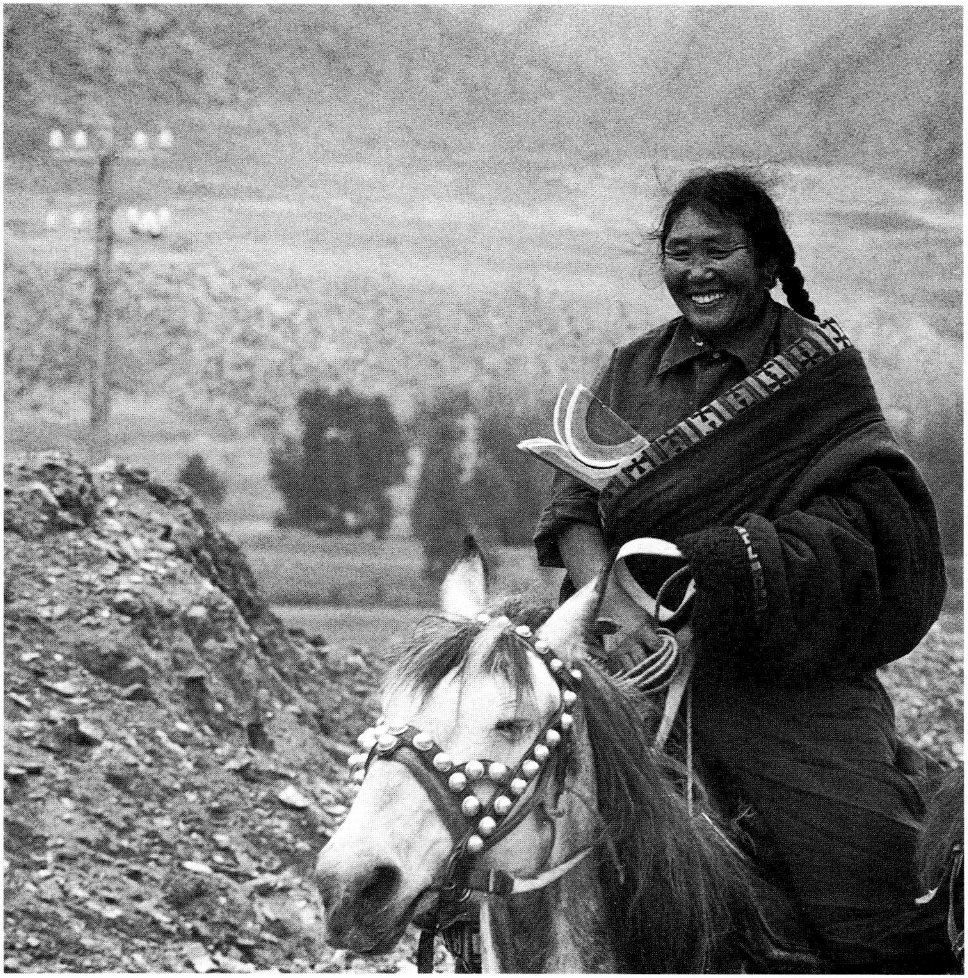

LEAVING XIAHE ON THE ROAD TO THE PLAINS

When we reached the lake, pure and shining,
like a mirror of itself
in sheer joy we jumped down, swirled round and round
so our clothes belled out and graced the silt
with a circle which we defined:
Our space
Mine
which I hadn't done since we were bairns
in gym-shoes.

(and I recalled the last town we'd passed,
en fête, where jugglers and acrobats
called a crowd around
but its centre was their stage.
In that dirty township
                    I hid my face
behind a fluttering fan,
of Queens and Aces,
so by the angry hiss of a
hurricane lamp
in the back of a chop-house
lost and won a pretty sum
and some I tossed to a blind beggar,
some a pick-pocket filched
and three gold coins I saved
for out the corner
                    of my eye,
behind my winning hand I'd seen
a wandering holy-man and part-time diviner.

Whose little fire rose scented
smoke into the sky, along the shore.

The joyous lake

turned coral, jasper in the gloaming,
a heron beat its languid wings,
though he called them back, shore-birds
flashed, were gone;

a woman in silhouette
arranged some silvered shards
on a granite boulder
then played a reed pipe
over the water

and with these folk Fa-hsien
devoured a meal,
shared travellers' nonsense,
risqué jokes,

until the mirror showed
the shepherd moon,
its scattered flock of stars.

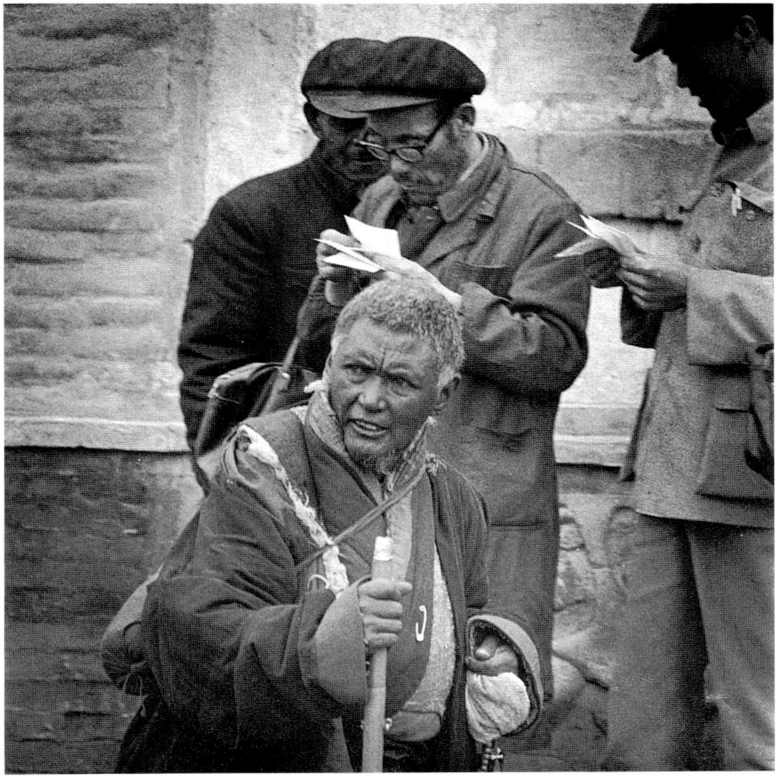

WANDERING MONK AT THE KUMBUM MONASTERY, TAERSI

Then I asked:
will we come this way again, this smiling lake?
And though the princess laid off playing
turned her back, we could feel
she was all ears when he warned
some things may never be resolved
then studied my upturned hand.

My cross-hatched palm: lines straight
as a cormorant's flight
                                        like an arrow shot
slow over the silent loch

said all that was past was lost
and there was everything to come

Set a stout hert tae a stey brae
                    he winked (a wink that showed
he wasn't so old he couldn't
follow home a twisting road
with a click of his heels,
wouldn't resist
                              a backward glance
to see who followed this ridiculous dance
through many people's many tongues.)

A sharp and sudden wind
forced between loch and sky
as if from under an ill-fitting door

as the princess tossed the coins
through heads and tails

and even she who'd snorted 'truth?
a game of spot-the-ball'

grew serious
as bracken shook, horses stamped
the troubled loch sent waves ashore,

scattered the diviner's cards,
our faces there.

Calm: and Fa-hsien took a twig
drew in the dust the coins' revelation

spoke to a place at the centre of us all:
the fire's core,

described a future in a measured tone:
if she'd be true

to her mirror
cracked, her inner loch, that humble heart,

the great force of that keen wind: her name
would be revered.

*

We saw him once more: in the dusty dawn
a distant home-turned figure
jaunty as a fiddler
down the loch-side dirt track.

As we saddled up, ready for the last push,
wondering again what kind of place it was
we rode toward
                    with a new resolve.

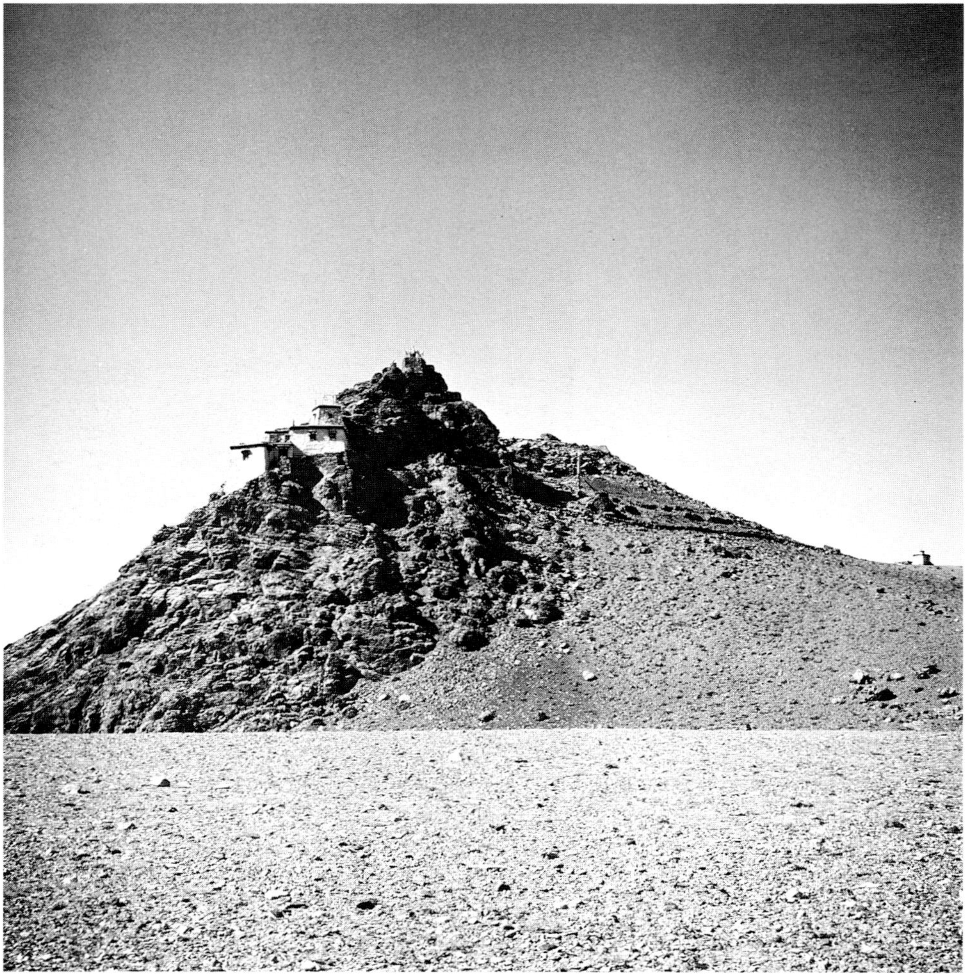

MONASTERY BY THE SHORES OF LAKE MANASAROVAR, WEST TIBET

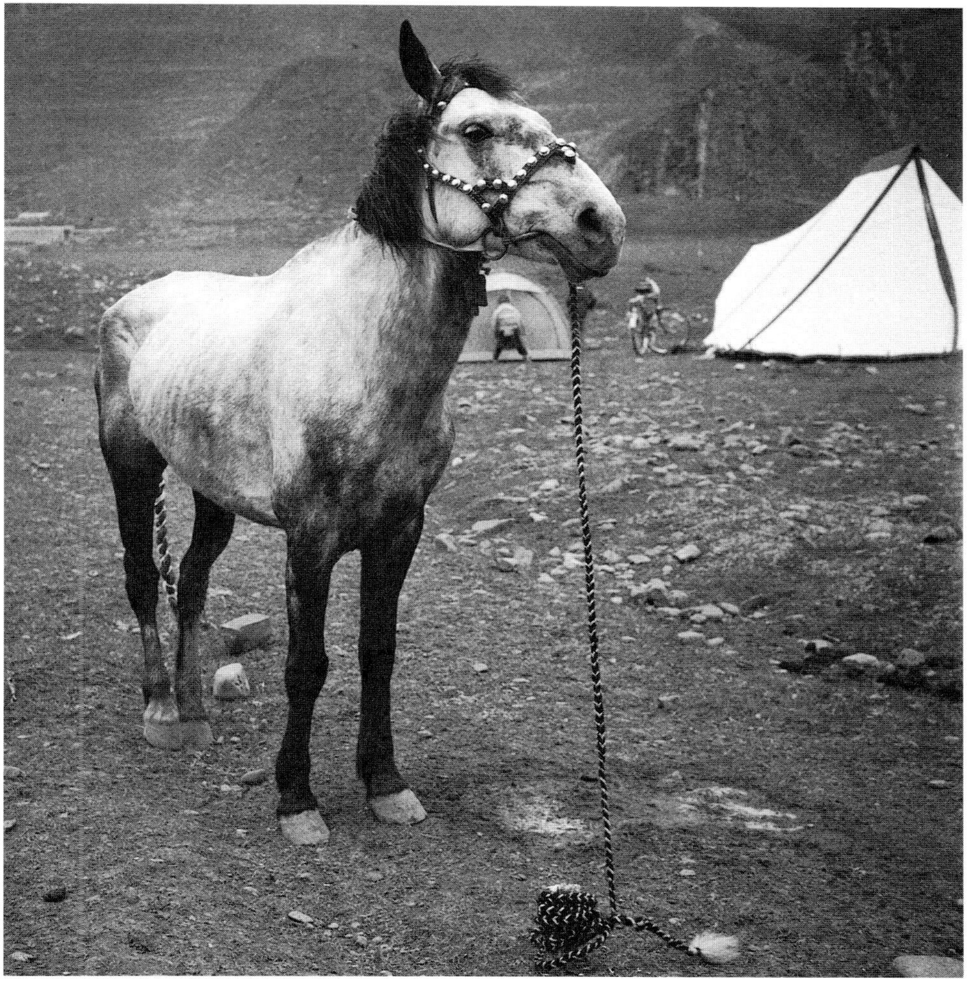

TETHERED HORSE AT THE HORSE FESTIVAL, XIAHE

The Panchen Lama rides from Lhasa to Kumbum

(A thousand miles in a single night)

Now the sky is saddled with stars,
a saddle of stars thrown over the hills' back;
night is a horse leaping the mountains,
night is a nomad shifted by morning,
the Panchen Lama rides hard out of Lhasa
low and clung to the horse's mane,
clings to the mane strung like a comet,
and clear of the darkened back-streets chants
to the ready ear, pale as a conch shell
the thousandth tantra's thousandth cycle,
and horse and Lama quit their earthly forms.

That night a wind crossed snow and pasture:
ruffled the feathers of sleeping rivers,
whirled like a cloak round the shoulders of mountains.
The plateau of Tibet
stretched away like an oil-dark painting
to the grass-land, where in tethered yurts
families wrapped in yaks-wool, slept;
and warm-flanked yaks shifted in their dreaming,
and certain dogs
who opened their jaws to the flying hoof-beat
with an invisible gesture of the Lama's hand
were silenced and charmed.

So for a thousand miles:
till the sun coaxed the world to open like a daisy;
splashed gold on the roofs on the gold-rooved monastery,
of the far side of the precious and protecting hill
at will assumed their mortal shape,
and the youngest boy-monk who rushed from the temple,
his face as round as a gong of wonder
to touch the robe, grab the reins, receive a blessing
and though that boy lived to be a hundred
he always swore
the Panchen Lama
winked.

(This is no story, desperate and apocryphal,
the horse is rumoured to be divine.)

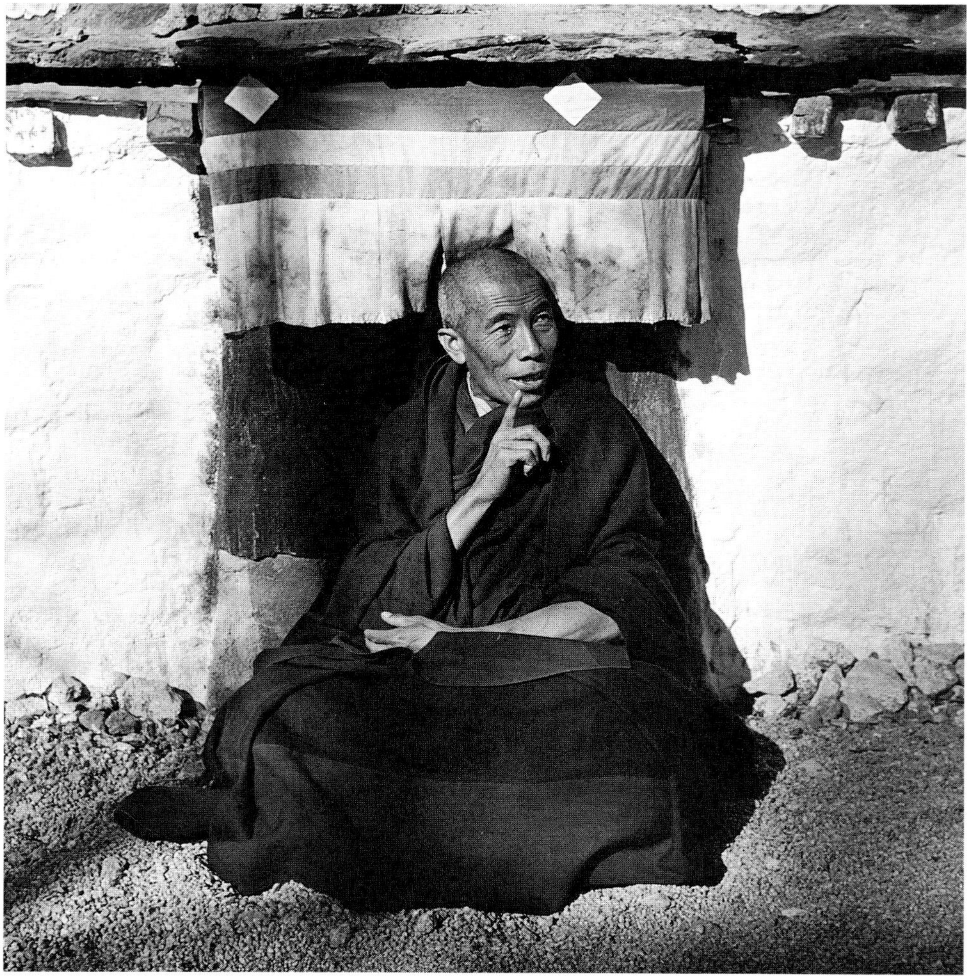

MONK IN THE COURTYARD OF THE SERA MONASTERY, LHASA

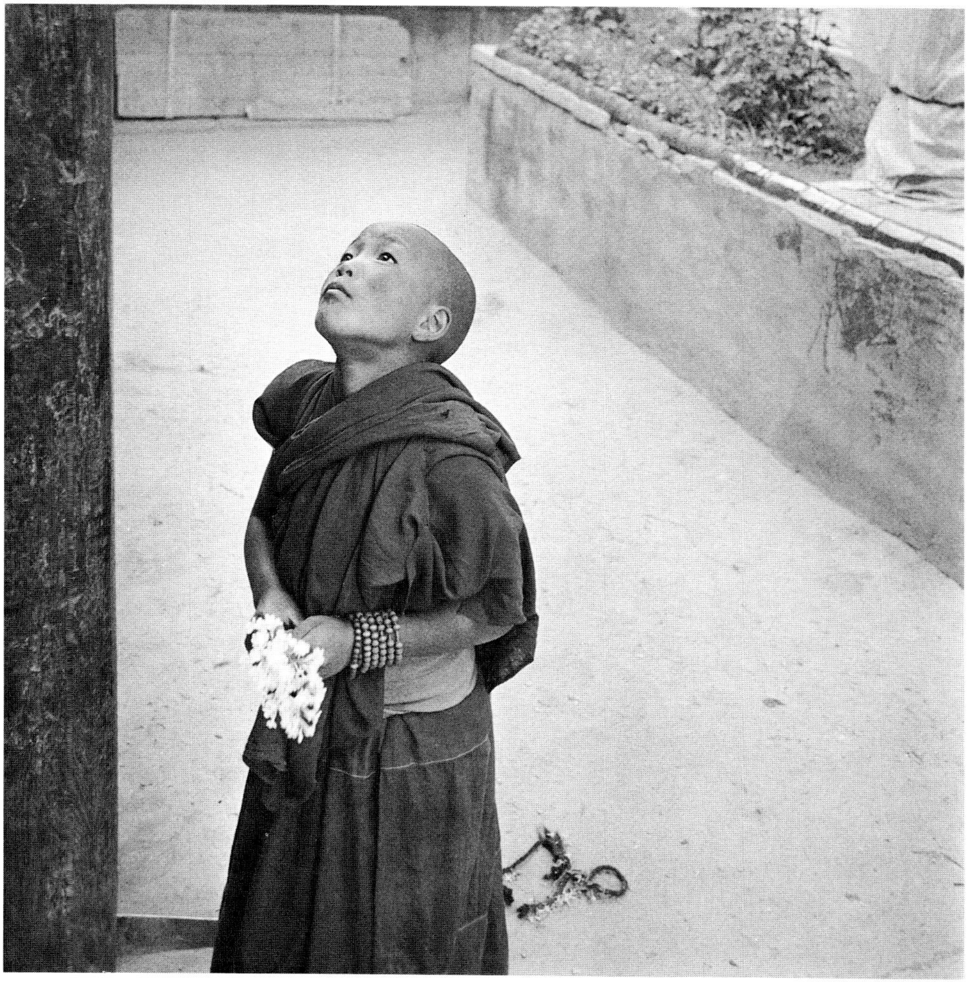

NOVICE MONK IN THE LABRANG MONASTERY, XIAHE

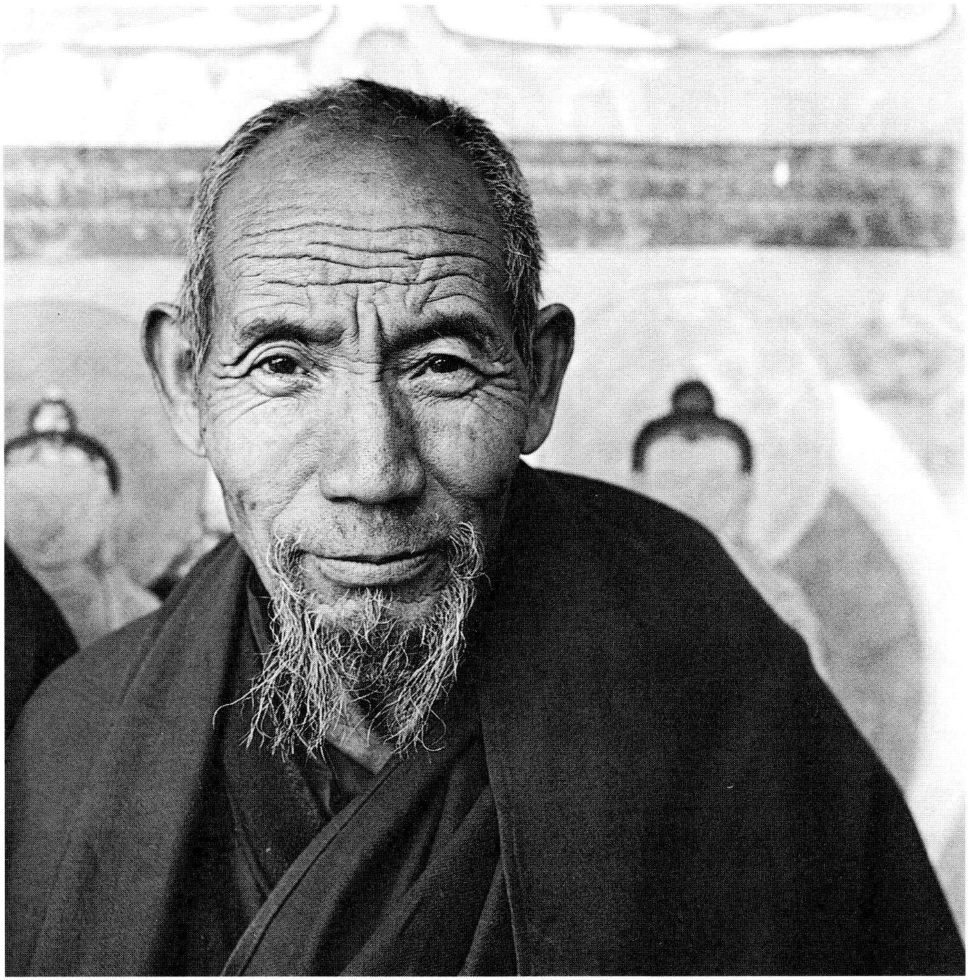

OLD MONK IN THE TASHILUMPO MONASTERY, SHIGATSE

As the Lama rode to the golden roofs
so the rays of the sun lead to the golden sun
so the wild stories come together
round a burning campfire
and the pewter path over the grassland
is a straight track.
So we are come. We turn over the stones
of the past as if reasons
and beginnings scuttled beneath,
and the rumours we repeat to ourselves
converge on truth.
The desert spoke in false voices tho' alluring,
but we can close the door softly and be gone,
with what we own
we must carry and bear.
And our horse mayn't be divine,
we must ride it and be astonished and glad
to arrive at a clutter of gold roofs
cupped in a valley:
with a scented tree
whose every leaf
shimmers with the face of the divine.

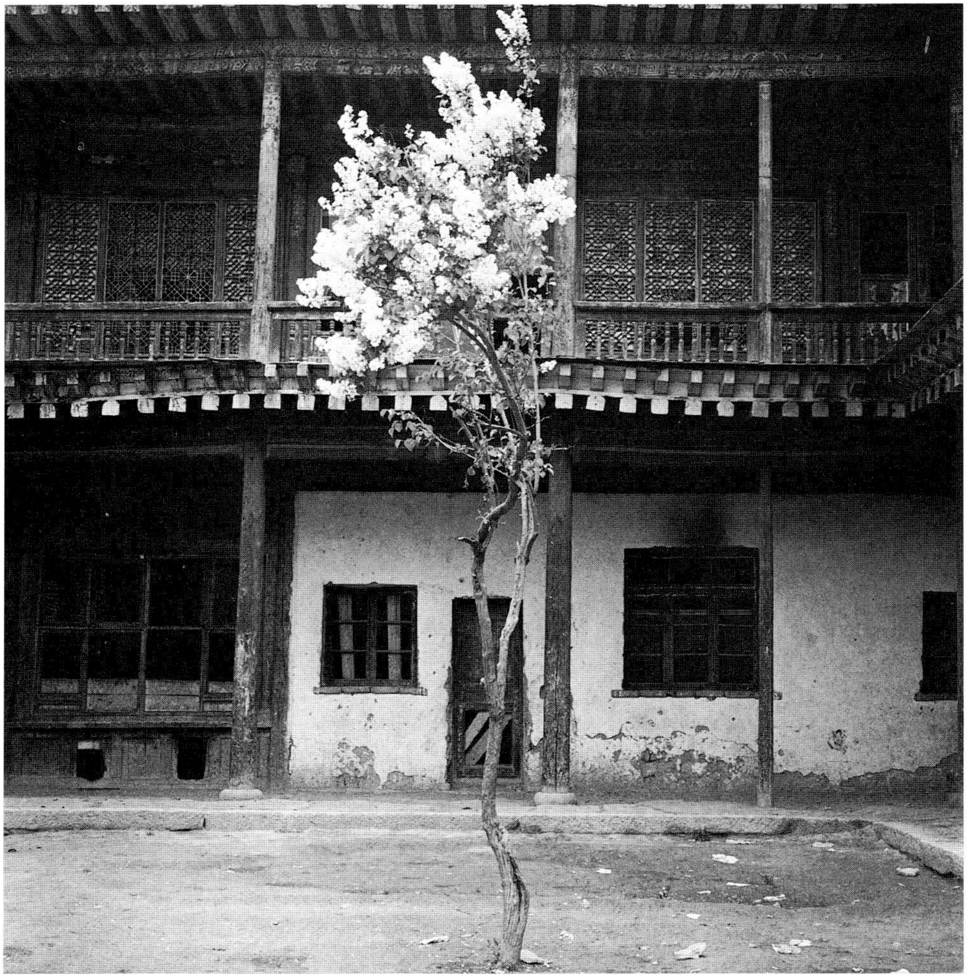

TREE IN A DESERTED MONASTIC BUILDING, XIAHE

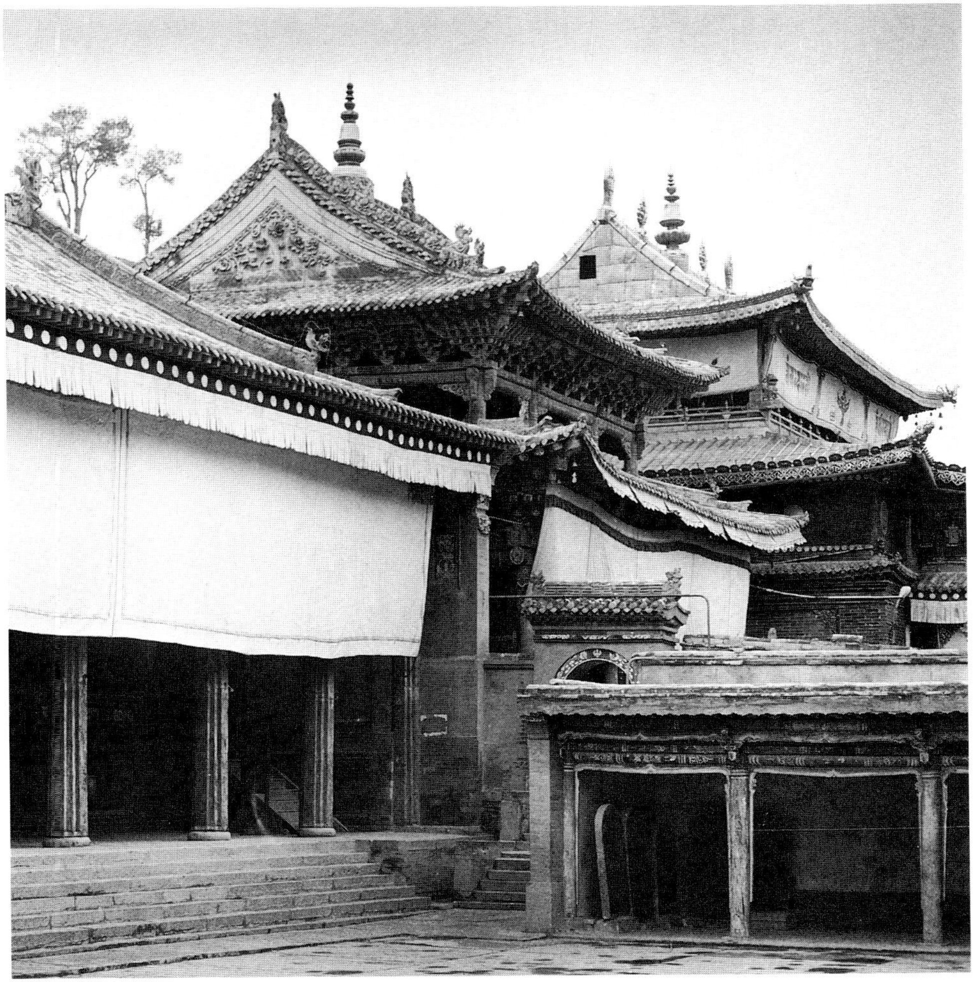

COURTYARD AND ROOFS, THE KUMBUM MONASTERY, TAERSI

For Paola

A boomin echo doon the corridor,
her door's the only ane open

lik a shell, an a wumman sweepin:
saft soun, wings.

A licht-bulb, hingit fi the ceilin
by a short cord.

A slever o gless in the oose
an a black hair. she telt me

they've killed 5000 people in Beijing.
Nou this wumman's haunin her gear

brushes an pens, her worn claes
for me tae cairry. But she'd a bin waitin

when they cam, chewin her gum
blawn them a bubble size o China.

This is a place your friens disappear:
trust naebody. Luve a.

The smearit wa's o a concrete room,
a wumman sweepin.

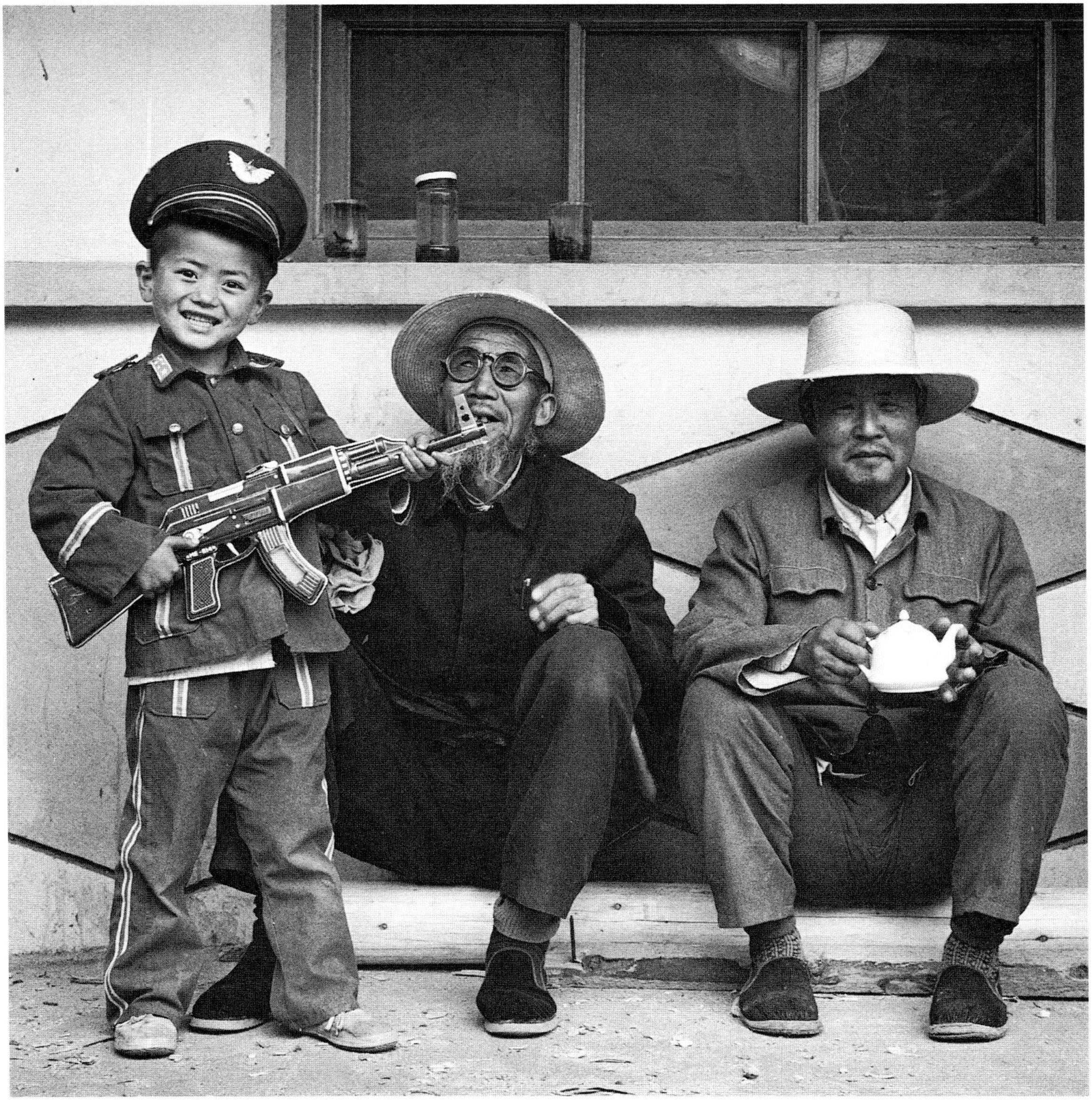

CHINESE TAKING TEA, XIAHE

Sang o the blin beggar

This is the dynasty o wickitness –
grieve agin the nicht an howl wi dugs

Great buildins murn thir ugliness –
dugs are scroungin politicians born again

the stars grow dangerous; they ken the script
o constellation's no thir ain

Folk that talk lik rivers o risin
will be swept awa tae gutters lik the rain

o this dynasty o wickitness
grieve agin the night and howl wi dugs.

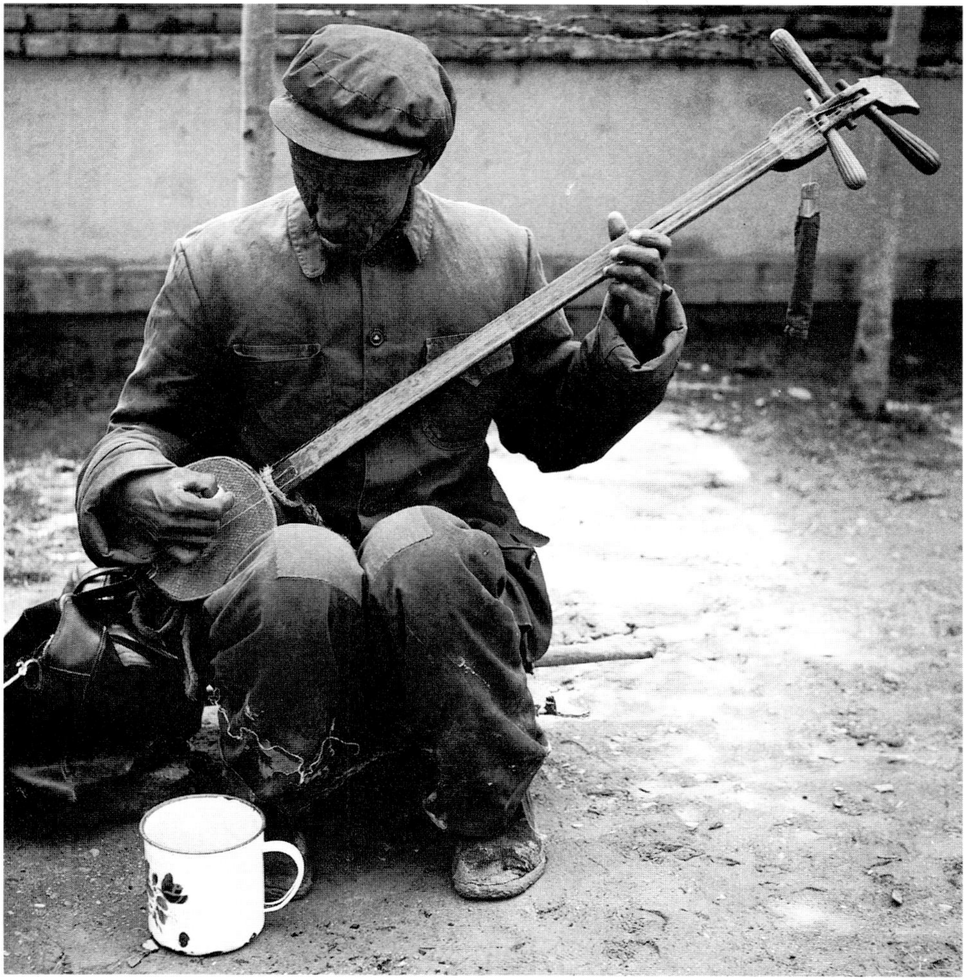

PILGRIM BEGGAR WITH HOME-MADE LUTE AT THE KUMBUM MONASTERY, WEST TIBET

The art-students

The art students say it's like breathing,
breathing,
and never being able to exhale.

The rain was pitiless.
From room to room, tongue
to tongue, our news is in Chinese whispers.

In the only hotel
permitted to foreigners
we tap the windows like flies.

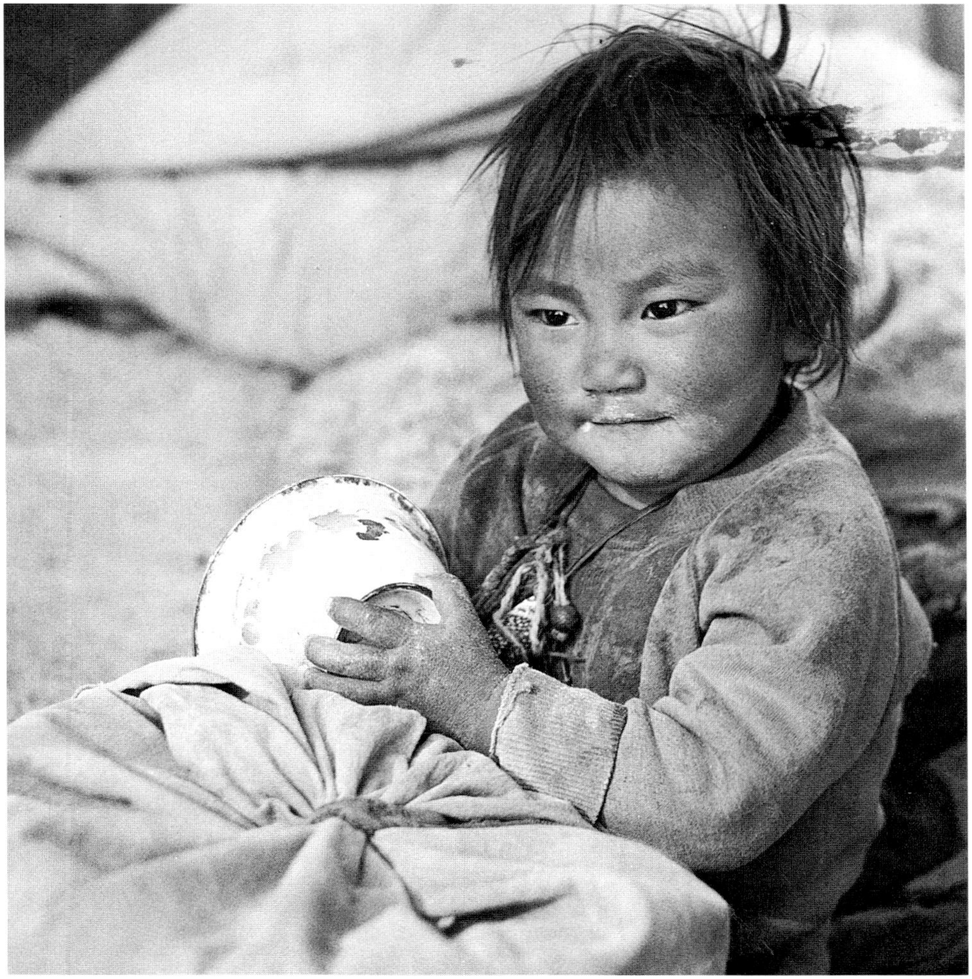

NOMAD CHILD ON PILGRIMAGE, WEST TIBET

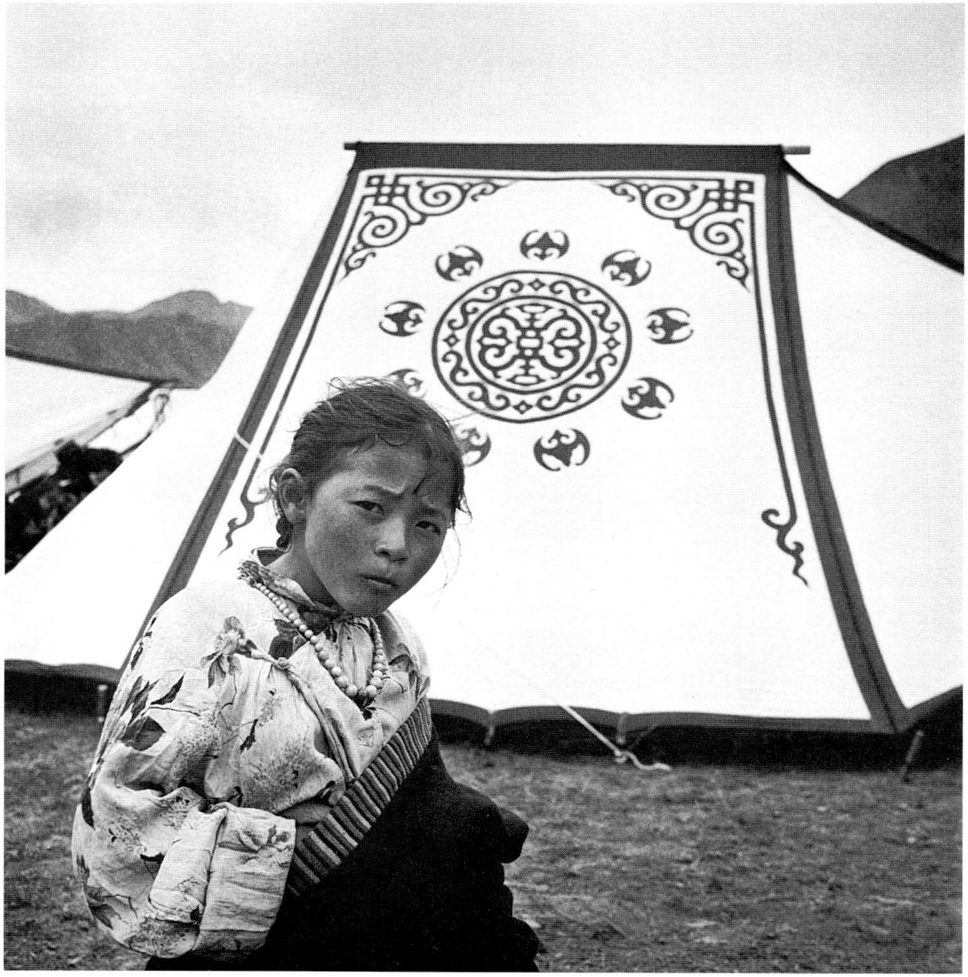

NOMAD GIRL AND TENT AT THE HORSE FESTIVAL, XIAHE

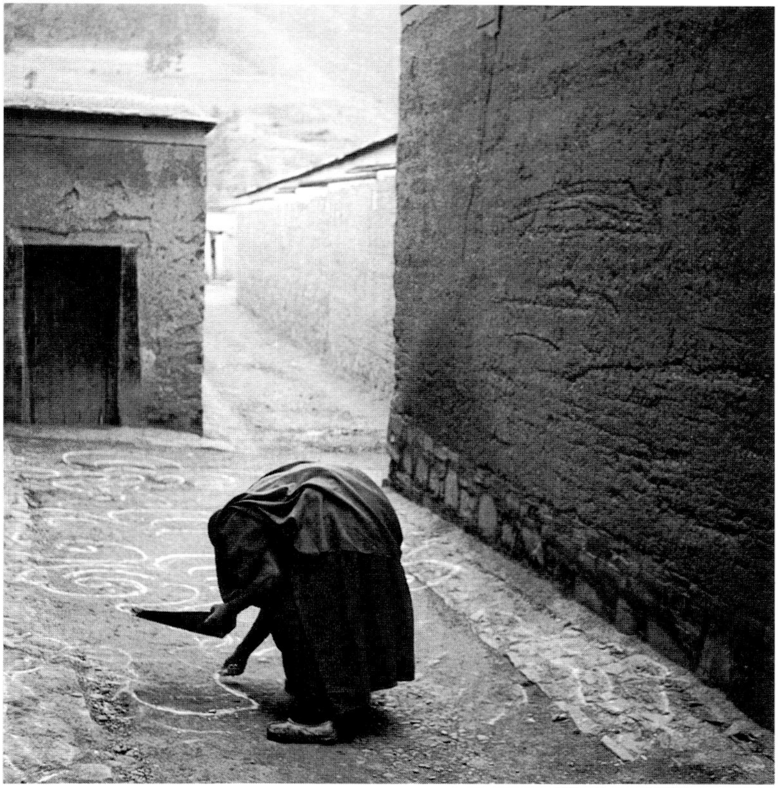

MONK MAKING RITUAL PATTERNS IN THE MONASTERY GROUNDS,
LABRANG MONASTERY, XIAHE

Xiahe

Abune the toon o Xiahe
a thrast monastery,
warn lik a yowe's tuith.

The sun gawps at innermaist
ingles o wa's.
Secret as speeders

folk hae criss-crosst a saucht
seedit i the yird flair
wi rags o win blawn prayer.

Xiahe. Wave droonin wave
on a pebbly shore,
the *ahe* o machair, o slammach,

o impatience; ahent the saft saltire
i trashed, an sheep;
wha's drift on the brae

is a lang cloud's shadda.
the herd cries a wheen wirds
o Tibetan sang,

an A'm waukenet, on a suddenty mindit:
A'm far fae hame,
I hae crossed China.

Xiahe (pronounced *Shi-ah-e*) a Tibetan town in the now Chinese province of Gansu; **sauch**: willow; **yird**: earth; **slammach**: cobweb.

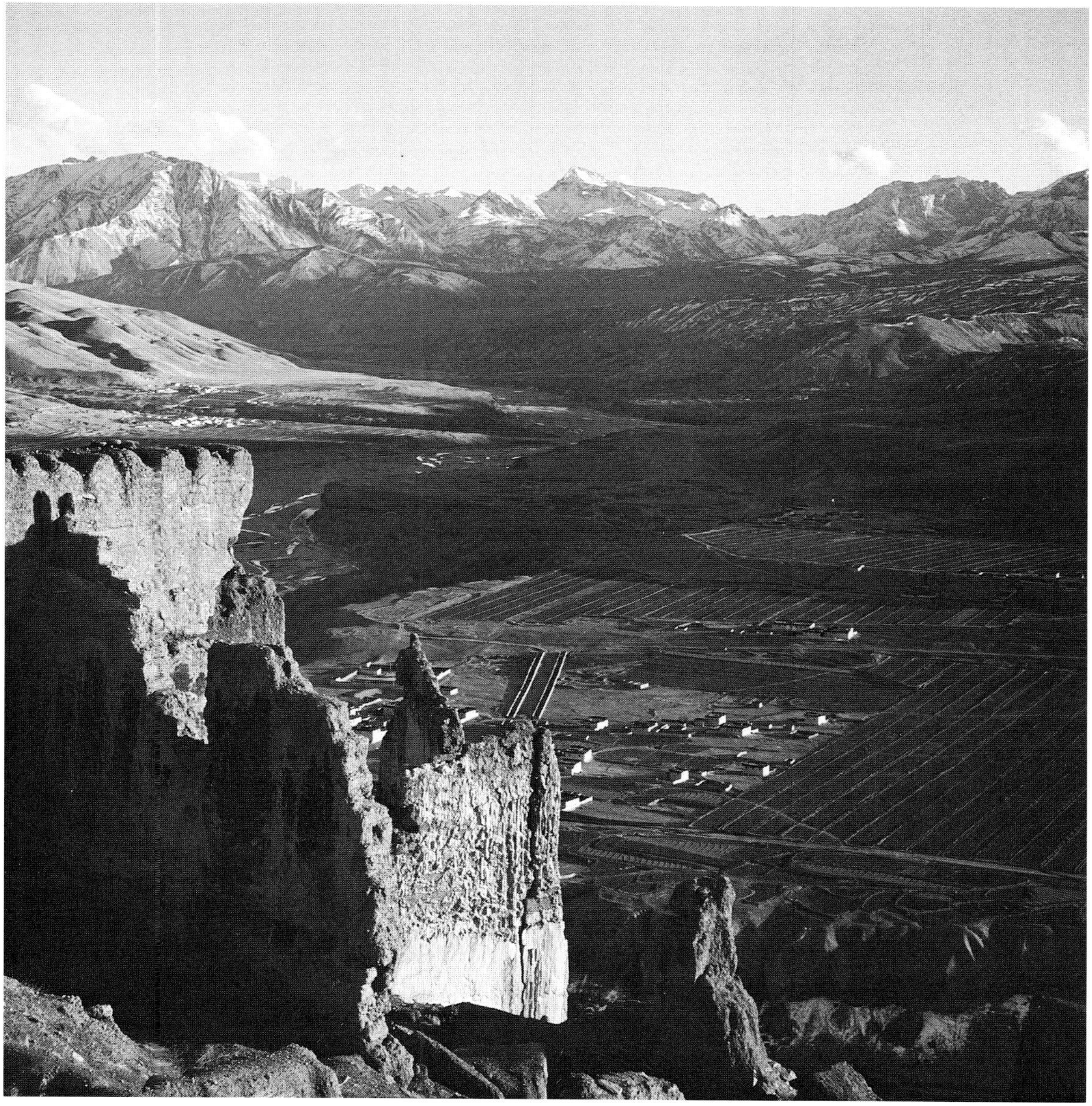

THE RUINS OF SIMBILING MONASTERY OVERLOOKING THE TOWN OF BURANG IN WEST TIBET